INCREASING
PERSONAL EFFICIENCY

The Psychology of Personal Progress

INCREASING
PERSONAL
EFFICIENCY

DONALD A. LAIRD, PH.D., SC.D.

FOURTH EDITION

Harper & Brothers, Publishers · New York

Personal efficiency depends greatly
upon loyalty to work and joy in work.
From one person more than all others
I have learned this by example and precept,
hence this book is dedicated

BY A SON

TO HIS MOTHER

TABLE OF CONTENTS

7117

INCREASING
PERSONAL EFFICIENCY

THIS IS NOT A BOOK TO BE READ THROUGH IN AN EVENING, although the average reader could probably do so without hurrying. This is a book to be studied and USED. If it is read properly much help should be received from its pages; if not read properly it is just "another book."

To read the following pages properly only two chapters should be read a week. One chapter can be read Monday evening. On Tuesday and Wednesday evenings the Personal Progress Pointers at the close of the chapter should be read again and half an hour spent regularly in discovering how these can be applied to your own case. On Thursday evening the following chapter can be read, and the Personal Progress Pointers pondered on the two following days.

Every human can profit by rest and worship, and to this should the remaining day be devoted.

INCREASING
PERSONAL EFFICIENCY

CHAPTER I

THE MIRACLE OF MODERN EFFICIENCY

I

THIS is the age of applied science. On every hand there are mute but lasting witnesses of the wonderful strides the sciences have made to serve man in a useful way.

But have you ever paused to reflect that applied science and efficiency engineering are one-sided in their development? Man spends his energies in finding out how to get a ton of steel to go farther, a typewriter to wear longer, an automobile to run cheaper, a light to shine brighter — but little of his time or thought to the development of his own efficiency.

The extreme development of natural material resources and their conservation is paralleled by a pitiable neglect of human mental resources.

If one can measure how exceedingly wasteful and negligent in the use of our mental resources we are, almost complete failure in mental efficiency is evidenced each year by the confinement of sixty thousand of our men, women, and youth in hospitals as mental patients. This is not for one year only, but for year after year, apparently without end. Some one with a passion for figures has found that there are three times as many persons in hospitals with mental diseases as there are men, women, and children in the entire state of Nevada.

[1]

Twelve times as many institutions to care for mental patients as there are universities enrolled in the Association of American Universities indicates that the national balance in mental efficiency is not being struck properly.

It is the losses in mental efficiency from less spectacular and more normal causes that receive the attention of the applied psychologist. He does not spend much time with the person who imagines he is the Czar of the Russias or with the person who is fully convinced that his clothes and skin are of glass and that others can watch the operations of his internal organs. The applied psychologist works for the 99,680 people out of each 100,000 who are *apparently* normal. That is a large clientele to be served, but one greatly in need of the services of the youngest and, at the same time, one of the most spectacular of the applied sciences—applied psychology.

II

Physical prowess *used* to count for a great deal. When our remote relatives were living an arboreal existence, it was probably the strongest or the fastest that ruled the herd. Some animals seemed to select, as it were, a line of development that made monstrous organisms. They developed such enormous strength that shrubs, small trees, and all living things gave way at their approach.

But here we come face to face with the bogie—*one-sidedness*. These animals developed great bones and powerful muscles to which their brain was as a pin head in comparison. It was one-sidedness, with the disadvantage given the mental life. And what was the result?

In the museums of natural history, we see the bones of the mastodon, an elephant-like animal that is now extinct. Powerful as it was, the animal was no match in the struggle for existence with the smaller, less powerful

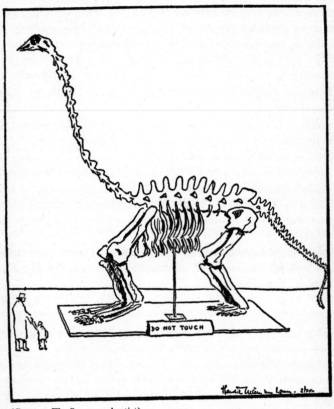

(Courtesy The Survey and artist)

ONE WAY TO MAKE HISTORY
Big bones

animals that had a brain less out of proportion to the bone and muscle.

Then there are ancient reptiles of gigantic size, so powerful that they could snap the trunk of a sapling with their tail. They were strong at one end but weak at the other. A tail with the strength of a Titan and a brain scarcely as large as your two fists. They could not compete successfully with animals that maintained an evener balance between the two ends. To-day they, too, are found only in museums and geological burying grounds. No monuments have been erected to their memory.

Were there such monuments they should be dedicated to the folly of one-sidedness. Only bones are left — the mind had been neglected.

Monuments are usually erected to commemorate accomplishments, not for bulk. Civilization remembers and bears the ineradicable mark of men who used their heads. It promptly buries and forgets those who did not use their brains along with their brawn.

Which way are you headed? Are you letting your brains look out for themselves? Remember the mastodon! Remember the dinosaur!

III

Bricklayers had been plying their trade for centuries when a psychologist dropped in for a few days. The old bricklayers laughed at him. If any living person were to know how to lay bricks, it would be a bricklayer. But the psychologist was not to be discouraged by derision. He looked on for a few days and then left.

Soon he returned with a motion picture camera and took pictures of the best bricklayers at work. Then he took the film to the laboratory and studied it, picture by picture.

The bricklayers had the time of their lives. Here was some educated fool who had never laid a row of bricks in

[4]

his life, looking at pictures and preparing to tell *them* how to do their work. They had always thought scientists were queer. Here was proof.

What did the applied psychologist, the educated fool with the hundreds of pictures, find? After he had studied the pictures, it was his turn to laugh. He had found that the average bricklayer was making eighteen movements in laying each brick. He found that the same work could be accomplished in *just five movements!* He had not used his brawn in handling bricks and mortar, but he had used his brains. By using his brains to study the brawn of others, he had showed them how to treble their output.

Frank B. Gilbreth, who found out how to treble the output of bricklayers, died in the spring of 1924. He will be remembered for generations. Remember the mastodon? And the dinosaur?

IV

Along such lines as these, the applied psychologist plies his way. Always making a careful scientific study first, he then makes his recommendations. He does not proceed by guesswork. The researches of the laboratory psychologist are studied. If these are not sufficient he performs experiments of his own. Guesswork is not to be tolerated.

The result is that the applied psychologist has accumulated a fund of information of amazing practical value. Most people are going through their day's work much as the bricklayers were. They do not seem to realize that their output can be greatly increased, whether they work with hands or with head. It is not going to be increased by laboring frantically and working oneself into a frenzy of activity. Just a simple trick here, the proper order there, thinking the right thing and doing it the right way.

Are you doing it the right way? We can tell as our book unfolds.

V

The applied psychologist is justly proud of his achievements. Some, perhaps with lofty intentions, have set themselves up as "practical psychologists" when they could not pass a sophomore examination in the subject. Although they may have laudable intentions, these near-charlatans are doing much harm in *preaching* their opinions and fantastic, unfounded notions. They are reaping a great profit from the overcredulous who are taken in by high-sounding phrases and promises of beauty, wealth, power, and perpetual happiness.

Bona fide psychology can accomplish everything that these cults can and have testimonials to spare. The bona fide applied psychologist can tell you the most efficient way to use your mental capacities and abilities. *Nobody else can, scientifically.*

Applied psychology is not inspirational at its source. It is scientific. But that does not imply that it is lacking in inspirational value. There is nothing more inspiring and stimulating than the laboriously unfolded truths about the workings of the human mind, its limitations, and its almost limitless possibilities. Inspiration that is founded on the cold facts of science possesses a double value. It is inspiration that has its feet on earth; it is inspiration that is within possibility, not the inspiration that is beyond realization and which brings only disappointment and failure.

You have your desk and your office equipped with efficiency-increasing appliances. You put attachments on your car that will increase its efficiency. Here is a personal question: *Have you given as much attention to your personal mental efficiency? Are you laying your mental bricks with eighteen movements or with five?*

CHAPTER II

THE EFFICIENT ENVIRONMENT

WHAT you accomplish in this world depends upon several things. One is the nature of the abilities with which you are born. A second is whether or not you use these abilities in the most efficient way. A third factor is the conditions under which you use your abilities.

You cannot be told by psychology how to be born with certain abilities. This chapter will be devoted to finding out what surroundings, conditions of light, temperature, ventilation, and health will do most to further your efficiency.

I

Colleges have often been subject to criticism because of the enormous sums spent by them in erecting their buildings. But recent experiments by Dr. Warner Brown at the University of California show that this money has not been squandered.

He had students take tests of mental work. Half of the students did the work in a dingy, attic-like room, while the other half were given the same work tests in an attractively furnished room. Those in the dingy room were neither able to do as much work nor do it as efficiently as the group working in the pleasing room.

It may be that geniuses can work best in an attic room littered with dirt, but such a condition shows that they are the exception that proves the rule. The rest of mankind can work better in attractive surroundings.

Fortunately our surroundings can largely be selected or altered to suit our needs.

What estimate would you place on the working value of your surroundings? In my workroom at the laboratory here I have curtains, potted flowers, and attractive, fresh paint. Window curtains and flowers seem rather out of place in a laboratory. But the truth of the matter is that they are exceedingly *in place*, although they are not common. Whether I am experimenting, writing, working over data, or conferring with students, the appearance of the room increases my efficiency.

Some rooms radiate the spirit and desire for work — others suggest Saturday night and spring housecleaning.

II

How well one works depends to a great extent upon how well the work is lighted.

Even illumination should be the first aim. Our eyes have developed through centuries of natural lighting in which contrasts are not marked. Nature cannot be improved upon by introducing uneven lighting.

When reading or sewing or doing any similar work, your room should be lighted as uniformly as possible. Table lamps, floor lamps, and desk lamps may be attractive but you should not depend upon these for illumination except when talking, listening to music, or resting. Whenever you are using your eyes except in the most casual way, you must have even, uniform lighting.

How much light is needed? The surface upon which you are using your eyes should be as brightly lighted as if there were ten candles one foot away. If the room has light-colored walls less illumination will be needed.

You can calculate for yourself how large the lamps should be. The first calculation is to find how many square feet there are in the room. The room in which I am writing, for example, is 18 by 23 feet, which makes the floor area 414 square feet.

Next the square feet must be multiplied by a *factor* which will give the watts necessary to produce adequate illumination. This factor varies, of course, with the color of the walls and the kind of lighting fixture used. The following table will show the factor for your own room:

	Light ceiling, light walls.	Light ceiling, dark walls.	Dark ceiling, dark walls.
Fixture with light-colored shade sending most of the light down....	2.5	2.9	3.1
Indirect fixture or one in which the light bulb is completely enclosed..	4.5	5.6	9.0

The room in which I am working has a light ceiling and light walls, so the factor is found in the first column. The fixtures are of the indirect type so the factor is the bottom one, that is, 4.5. Now the total area of 414 square feet is multipied by this factor of 4.5 which gives 1,863 watts. This means that I should have bulbs to total 1,863 watts. What I have is six bulbs of 300 watts each.

This lighting scheme consumes a great amount of current, but I am using my eyes twelve hours a day in this room and my eyes and work are worth more than the electricity. And the added work I do more than repays for the cost of the electricity. When I first occupied the room, there

[9]

were four lamps of 60 watts each for illumination. My eyes hurt and I was tired after a few hours' work. I soon had the lighting changed and can now work in comfort and without fatigue.

How about your study or sewing room? Let me do some calculating. It is probably 9 by 12 feet, which makes a floor space of 108 square feet. You probably have a light shade on the lamp which directs the light toward the floor. From the table we find the factor — if there are light walls — to be 2.5. This means that you should have 260 watts in bulbs. I would wager that you do not have 100!

Make a note right now to get bulbs that will correctly light your workroom. You will thank me for this, for I am thinking of your personal efficiency.

Before you get these additional bulbs you must be warned against the harm of using ones in which the white-hot wires can be seen by the eye. If you have a fixture in which this filament is completely hidden, then get clear glass bulbs. If, however, your fixtures do not entirely obscure this filament, then you should get white-enameled bulbs.

The irritating, fatiguing, white-hot filament is a potent source of lessened efficiency. Avoid it entirely, not only in your workroom but in every room in your house.

If your neighbor should go outdoors and gaze with un-protected eyes at the sun, it would not be long before he would be blinded. Still you are probably looking at several miniature suns every evening in your rooms. Every uncovered lamp filament is a miniature sun.

Not every room in the house should be as brightly illuminated as by ten foot-candles. Or rather, perhaps they should be but it might prove to be expensive. The bench in the basement or garage and the room where the evening paper or the correspondence course is read should have ten foot-candles illumination. And the kitchen and sewing room should be lighted similarly.

How many of these specifications can your place pass? It is my recommendation that you see it meets every one as quickly as possible. It will pay, as it paid one factory in increasing its earnings 10 per cent.

III

There is another fact about vision that you should know. The odds are not quite even that you need glasses, if not all the time at least when reading or doing any similar eye work.

Henry Ford found recently that almost half of his workmen had defective vision. And of course you know of Theodore Roosevelt's experience with his eyes and what glasses meant to him. Headaches, fatigue, and inefficiency are oftentimes due to slightly defective eyes. In almost every case glasses will remedy the trouble.

In the telephone directory you will find listed an oculist, or an optometrist, or a physician who specializes in diseases of the eye, or in fitting glasses. Telephone for an appointment to have your eyes examined. You may want your personal physician to recommend someone to you, but make certain you go to someone licensed for this special work and who makes dealing with eyes his chief business.

If you need glasses the total cost may be $15 to $20 but they will be worth a thousand times that to you. If you do not need glasses: Remember the story of the man who would not fix a leaky roof because when it was raining he could not fix it, and when there was no rain there was no leak?

IV

Do you remember the ditty which went:

"What is it moulds the life of man?
     The weather.
What makes some black and others tan?
     The weather.
What makes the Zulu live in trees,
And Congo natives dress in leaves,
While others go in furs and freeze?
     The weather."

The weather is more than an ever-ready topic for talk. It has important influences upon the amount of work one can do.

A banker told me recently that he could not understand what happened to his clerks in the summer. Clerks who made no mistakes in their computations during the winter months were unable to keep their books free from error in the summer.

It *is* almost impossible to keep from making mistakes in such mental work as this during the summer. Errors increase with each rise in the temperature until at a temperature of 90 degrees there are 60 per cent more mistakes than on average days.

Why this is still puzzles scientists, but it is of immense practical importance, whether or not we completely understand why. The decrease in efficiency may be due to uncomfortableness, or it may be due to changes in the metabolism of the body. Van't Hoff's law of chemical action states that chemical activity increases as the temperature rises. It is thought by Professor Putter that high temperatures increase the chemical activities in the body faster than oxygen can be absorbed to oxidize the waste products. The accumulation of these waste products produces effects that are the same as those of fatigue, and bodily efficiency is consequently lowered.

Efficiency falls when the temperature goes much above 68 degrees Fahrenheit. Both mental and muscular work is lessened either in quality, or quantity, or both, at temperatures even slightly above this point. When it is below 48 degrees human efficiency also begins to fall. The temperature of 68 degrees is generally considered the best for health as well as for efficiency.

From New England south to Florida, strength and health and efficiency vary with the temperature of the seasons. Dr. Ellsworth Huntington, of Yale University, has found that neither the summer nor the winter is the best time for work. Around October in the fall and April in the spring human machines seem to work most efficiently, just as an automobile engine has a certain temperature range for its most efficient and powerful working. Factory workers, military and naval cadets, cotton-mill workers, cigarmakers, and steel-mill workers have been found to be like the gas engine in having certain optimum temperatures for work.

It may be only accidental that income tax blanks are to be filled out in a month in which few mathematical mistakes are made and in which efficiency is high. It may be purely accidental, too, that inventories and fiscal reports are made in the winter months. In all these cases, however, the accuracy of the work is increased by the time of year selected. Inventories and fiscal reports would be further benefited in the temperate zones, though, if they were not made in January but in April, May, or September, for fewest errors are made in these three months.

The effects of bad working weather may persist for some time. An extremely hot summer, for instance, has been observed to produce injurious effects on work that persist for a considerable time after the weather has moderated. Returned missionaries may require years to regain their maximum efficiency.

Mark Twain said that climate lasts all the time and weather a few days. This fickleness of weather furthers human efficiency. The feminine characteristic of weather — changeableness — appears to increase efficiency. When the temperature is the same from day to day, it has been found that the work one does gradually declines. A study of the way 2,500 people are influenced by the weather has shown that a change in weather, whether for better or worse, favors better work and more work.

It is conceivable that the salesman who passes from a warm store or office into the lower temperature outdoors on his way to another prospect has his efficiency increased. His business makes variable weather for him.

Many schools have fresh-air drills in which the windows are thrown open and cool outside air admitted. Probably it is the purity of the outside air that aids the health of the children. It is the stimulation of a change in temperature among other things that furthers their working efficiency. In many universities the janitors open the classrooms between lectures so that at the opening of the lecture the room is cool. This change in temperature is beneficial.

I know a scientific worker who keeps the temperature of his laboratory as close to 65 degrees as possible all the time. This is a good working temperature. He always has his rooms ventilated by two windows that the janitor opens slightly the first thing in the morning. Many times during the day I have watched this man cross the room to one of these partly opened windows and examine a specimen closely. At other times, when he is working on a manuscript, I have seen him go to one of the open windows to think over the next passages. Without realizing why he does so he has greatly improved his working efficiency by changing his external temperature from the uniform 65 degrees to a lower temperature by the cool draft from the window. He never has a cold and is an indefatigable worker.

[14]

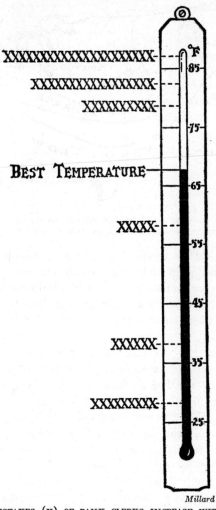

Millard

HOW THE MISTAKES (X) OF BANK CLERKS INCREASE WITH THE TEM-
PERATURE. (WHAT DOES YOUR THERMOMETER SAY NOW?)

Millard

HOW MENTAL EFFICIENCY IS HELPED BY THE WEATHER. (MOST OF OUR
GREAT UNIVERSITIES ARE IN THE "HIGH" BELT.)

All life seems to be stimulated by a variable temperature. Plants do not grow well in unusually high or low temperatures. Neither do they grow best in a uniform temperature. The best condition for their growth is when there are *slight* variations from hour to hour around an optimum temperature.

Moist air furthers efficiency. *Too* moist or "muggy" days have the opposite effect. Muggy days are inefficient because they are hot as well as moist. On any but hot days, a high humidity is very desirable.

If the weather does not favor one with the proper amount of moisture, it can be supplied by artificial means. In winter the heating apparatus should be modified in some way to offset the drying influences of the heat generated. The usual method followed by the householder is to put a pan of water on a stove or other heating apparatus. The pans that are built in hot-air furnaces are most effective, however, and raise the humidity in the house by as much as 1 per cent. The usual indoor humidity in winter is

[16]

about 25 per cent, whereas it should be nearer 60 per cent for best working conditions. Any apparent benefits from the home-made humidity devices are largely due to suggestion. A length of wicking exposed to a current of air is perhaps the most efficient home humidifier.

At the present time civilization and temperature are hand in hand. Some regions have better weather conditions than others. England is favored in this respect. The average January temperature in London is 38 degrees and in June it averages 63 degrees. On the continent the seasonal variation is greater and the days below and above the optimum temperatures are numerous.

The Pacific Coast of the United States is ideal in many ways. Seattle has a temperature much like London. San Francisco weather is favorable to work after the fogs have passed away. The California climate inland is not so ideal, due to the heat which averages 82 degrees in Fresno in the summer. The favorable temperatures of England and the Pacific coast are largely due to the west winds that blow over them from the ocean.

The humidity of these same regions, which averages about 70 per cent, is also efficiency increasing. Japan is not only too warm but is also too damp to be ideal for work.

San Francisco is penalized because of its slight variation, which does not reach the optimum desirable of 10 degrees, and North Dakota is penalized because of its great changes.

It is not an accident that the people who lead civilization throughout the world, as well as in America, live in regions where the climatic conditions further their efficiency. The favorable working conditions have aided them in building their civilizations.

The temperature of our workrooms must be regulated closely. It should be kept between 60 and 70 degrees — better under 60 than above 70 degrees. How to dress in the winter offers a problem. You probably know of persons who wear heavy woolen underwear because it is cold outdoors, but who work in rooms that are heated as warm as during summer weather. In some cases, I should not be greatly astonished if a thermometer held between them and their red flannels would nearly reach the boiling point. Ventilation should start at the skin and end at the window. Of course, when one is promenading along the street in winter, flannels are comforting but one might as well throw the typewriters out of the office window as bring flannels in the door.

"The air smells bad in here." Well it may, but is bad-smelling air bad? What makes bad air bad?

As you breathe, oxygen is taken out of the air and carbon dioxide given off to replace it. And carbon dioxide is not healthful. The bad effects of air, however, are almost never, under *ordinary* circumstances, due to carbon dioxide. In deep mines and some types of factories, enough may accumulate to do harm, but in ordinary dwellings, workshops, and auditoriums rarely does such a condition arise.

Opening the window may make the air cooler but so far as removing poisons from the air, it is all unnecessary. Hygienists know this, but they urge persons to have open windows because they also know the tendency to dress too warm, have houses too warm, and sleep under too many bed clothes.

A startling experimental demonstration of this was first made in an European laboratory quite a few years ago. In one room of the laboratory workmen constructed a small, air-tight compartment, just large enough to contain a man. Openings large enough for a human head to be stuck through were made in the sides of the box. These were so built that they, too, were air-tight.

Into this coffin-like vault, one of the laboratory assistants was placed and the vault sealed. Once inside he rebreathed the air which became hotter and fouler with each breath. At last he felt about ready to faint and put his head through one of the openings to breathe the cool, pure air of the laboratory.

But did this revive him and prevent fainting? His lungs were breathing fresh air, but his body was encased in hot, moist air and the faintness and nausea persisted until his body was cooled.

When the man in the vault began to feel faint, some of the other laboratory workers put their heads into the vault through the other openings. Their bodies were exposed to the cool air of the laboratory but their lungs breathed and rebreathed the hot, foul air of the vault. Did they become faint? No, their bodies were cool. It is not the air in the lungs so much as it is the air around the body that plays havoc with our efficiency.

"Easy enough in the winter," you say, "but how about the summer?" Are you going to recommend that I carry a portable ice plant with me?" Well, some large manufacturers have found that it paid them to install special cooling chambers from which air is forced through ducts to the workrooms.

Cold air is not the only *cooling* air. When air is in motion, it cools your body just as effectively as does cold air that is motionless. The electric fan does not make air cold, but it makes air cool hot, tired, inefficient human beings by putting the air in motion.

Before the summer slump comes see that you have a fan to keep the air in your workrooms on the move. A fan is one of the cheapest electrical conveniences to operate, and a hot body is an inefficient condition to suffer.

You cannot keep your body surface breathing efficiently if you cover it with woolens in the summer months. Men can learn much from women in this matter.

V

How do you work under distractions? Probably better than under more favorable conditions.

This is because one seldom works his best and, when distractions interfere, he can rise to the occasion and work better than under usual conditions. There is a large margin separating what we really do from what we are able to do — and should do. The distractions show how great this margin is.

There are two worthy points in the matter of distractions. One is that you can do more than you usually do if there is the incentive. The other is that disturbances should be avoided; they are poor incentives.

Dr. John J. B. Morgan has shown the harmful effects of distractions. He found that one can do better work under distractions but that *more energy is needed* to get it done.

You can overcome all but the worst distractions, but to do so takes unusual effort and consumes extra energy. You can avoid this effort and conserve the energy by avoiding and eliminating the distractions.

What are some of the distractions you can eliminate? Do you face the window? That can be eliminated. Can you prevent doors slamming? And squeaks, loud talking, glaring light, bodily discomfort?

Look around now, find some distractions, and then rid yourself of them.

VI

When the telephone rings, the housewife has to send the children outdoors and hold her free hand over one ear before she can understand the electric voice. Distractions are no bother to her husband when he telephones in an office with typewriters and other office machinery going full tilt. He can talk across the continent without being disturbed.

These illustrations are not exaggerations. Once I used them in a talk, after which a man approached me and said, "My wife has had eight people stop work in my office every Wednesday afternoon for three years when she telephones home to see how the children are!"

Distractions are oftentimes due to your *inner attitude* rather than to the noises themselves. The woman who can hear only the noises of the house when she is telephoning will be deaf to these same sounds when she is reading an interesting novel. If one is interested, there is little danger of being distracted.

You are distracted because you do not want to listen or do not want to work. Watch yourself when you are engaged in work you like to do, or in talking to friends you like, and you will notice that you are not disturbed. People who are distracted are either bored or want to be disturbed.

If you find yourself easily distracted, acquire an interest in your work or take up more fascinating work. Try overcoming this inner attitude: later pages will help you.

VII

Recently I was talking with a young business man who staunchly maintained that a drink or two of wine increased his efficiency. Was he right?

He said that he felt keener, was wittier than ever, thought faster, and danced with more grace after a few drinks. But all the evidence he had was his memories of mildly intoxicated periods. A magistrate will not accept the testimony of one who is intoxicated. May we?

We do not have to, for the influences of alcohol upon the efficiency of human beings has been studied in the laboratory. Beer containing only 2.75 per cent of alcohol, for instance, has been found to make the hand less steady, the control of voluntary movements slower and less accurate, adding slower, and it retarded learning.

The amount of the loss in the tests varied directly with the amount of alcohol consumed. The loss in the more complex processes, such as learning and adding, lasted not longer than three hours after the drinking, while the losses in muscular power lasted much longer, even when small amounts of the 2.75 per cent beer had been consumed.

The 2.75 per cent beer also increased the pulse beat. The heart has enough to do without racing itself to an early death.

Rid yourself of the idea that alcohol and efficiency mix; they don't! The only good thing we can say for alcohol is that it produces a mild and more or less transient insanity.

VIII

Before an operation the surgeon sometimes takes a cup of black coffee; but coffee is forbidden children. An eminent Scandinavian scientist takes a cup of black coffee before tackling a stiff intellectual problem. The active drug in coffee is caffein. The average breakfast cup of coffee contains about 2.5 grains of caffein, while a cup of tea contains 1 grain less.

Carefully controlled experiments lasting for 40 days, in which the subjects did not know when they were getting caffein and when they were not, tell us conclusively some things about the action of this coffee drug on human beings.

A small dose of coffee affects one's control of muscles quickly. After a small dose of coffee one can use his muscles faster. And there is no depressing effect following this increase in quickness. An average dose of the coffee drug not only increases muscle speed but also increases the finer control over the muscles that is known as coordination. Thus fewer errors were made in typewriting after doses of caffein.

Coffee affects those processes that control muscular action first, and the effect quickly dies off, leaving no bad after effects.

Mental work is also stimulated by average-sized doses of the coffee drug. One can calculate quicker, name colors quicker, think quicker after taking coffee. These effects upon mental work do not appear as soon after imbibing as the changes in muscular control, but they last longer.

When coffee is taken with meals, the effect upon mental and muscular control becomes less marked. Small people are also affected differently than larger people by caffein.

The effect of being made "staggery" drunk by sipping coffee is not a natural phenomenon. In cases such as this, there is some mental trick being played, similar to that played on the person who is nauseated when he sees a red-headed person.

IX

What tobacco does to our efficiency is not definitely known. For some reason or another, it seems to be difficult for one to keep an impartial attitude in experiments with the divine weed.

Tobacco contains nicotine, which is a potent and harmful poison. In smoking, however, the burning changes the nicotine to a much less harmful drug known as pyridine. When tobacco is chewed, the nicotine remains nicotine.

Dr. J. P. Baumberger, of Stanford University, has studied the effects of tobacco smoking on a strenuous mental occupation in which telegraph operators were sending messages continuously all day long. He found that the heavy smokers accomplished less than the light smokers. Late in the day, when the pressure of the work increased, the

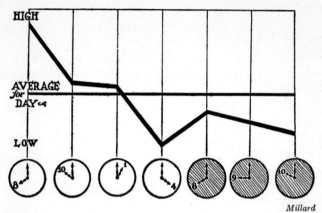

Millard

HOW MENTAL EFFICIENCY FALLS THROUGH THE DAY. THE AFTERNOON IS THE TIME FOR ROUTINE WORK, THE FORENOON THE TIME FOR NEW OR HARD WORK.

heavy smokers were not able to handle their full share of the work.

In some other cases a slightly beneficial effect has been found which has been attributed to tobacco. In so many other cases, however, it has been unequivocably found that tobacco lessens efficiency, that the best judgment is for one to "go light" on the weed.

X

What is the best time of day for working?

A famous scientist claims that he can do his best work only after sundown and he labors earnestly from then until long after midnight. Most people could do only the most mediocre mental work during these hours. This scientist, too, could have done better thinking at other hours if he had not got into the peculiar habit of using his brain at this certain time.

The kind of mental work that one can do varies definitely

[24]

from hour to hour of the day. Most people can do their best work in the morning. Every hour later there is a decrease in their working efficiency, until about eight o'clock in the evening when they probably revive slightly. The charts show how mental efficiency was found to fall during the day and rise and fall during the week.[1]

The longer one works, the less results are being obtained for the time and effort that is being expended. This loss in efficiency is not due to the time of day so much as it is to the hours one has already been at work. This loss of efficiency is found both in continued mental and in physical work, if they can really be divided. The laborer in the street who works mainly with his arms and shoulders suffers a loss in efficiency as the hours of work progress. The lawyer in his office who does mainly head work experiences the same loss.

When some folks think they can work only at some unheard-of time, they are really fooling themselves. They have formed certain habits of mental work to which they are enslaved. Such is the case with a modern woman poet, whose lines are eagerly read by thousands. She composed her poetry only when her feet were perched on a table and she was smoking a black cigar.

The cigar and the feet on the table are not essential for this mental work; they are the result of a habit. Thus it is also habit that makes the student believe that he can do his best by studying after ten o'clock in the evening. He is spending more time and getting his lessons less accurately than he would if he studied in the forenoon. But he, as have most of us, has become a slave to habit.

The business man who has routine work as well as mental work to do should delay the routine until afternoon. He should do the mental work in the morning if

[1] The data for these were gathered by Miss Bernice Appleby, a student of mine while I was at the University of Wyoming.

he is to be at his best. The most common tendency, however, is to delay the mental work until afternoon and get the easier work out of the way first. This is making the mental work really harder and defeating the end desired.

A foreign proverb says, "The morning hour has gold in its mouth." Every morning you have access to a gold mine, so gather every nugget!

XI

A vacation, according to the dictionary, is a change of occupation. Changing occupations has been found to increase the working ability of persons engaged in dexterous physical work, according to the recently announced findings of Dr. J. P. Baumberger, whose acquaintance we made on the subject of tobacco.

In work where there is a slight change in the task from time to time it was discovered that the actual working capacity was about 7.7 per cent below the maximum capacity, while in other tasks, which were continuous throughout the working, there was from 36.8 to 39.4 per cent loss from the maximum working capacity.

The findings indicate to Dr. Baumberger "that men working at alternating occupations have an output more closely approaching their maximum work capacity than do men in processes studied in which the same occupation was continued throughout the day.

"Some theoretical basis can be found for this when we consider the fact that fatigue is primarily within the central nervous system. Any change in occupation, although involving the same muscles, would necessarily involve different synapses and opportunity for recovery from fatigue for the previous group would be present."

Fatigue feelings can be overcome by changing to a

more interesting task. This is made possible since most fatigue is not genuine organic fatigue but merely "tired feelings." The interest replaces monotony and the feelings of fatigue quickly vanish.

This would be dangerous to do in some circumstances. Occasionally in physical work fatigue is real and not imagined. Further exertion might have harmful results under these conditions.

Even in cases of real fatigue, however, the fatigue is not spread over the entire body. Some slight effects of real fatigue are transferred over all of the body even when only a small group of muscles is used, but for most practical purposes these may be neglected. The greatest fatigue effects are found in the muscles that are involved in the work. If a change is desired to get around this fatigue, other muscles should be exercised and the fatigued ones given a chance to rest.

Fatigue from inserting letters in envelopes can be lessened by alternating with sorting or checking supplies. Mowing the lawn can be alternated with washing windows; beating rugs with dusting books. These activities are different enough to give a chance for real fatigue to be distributed.

In mental work it is likely that a change may always be a rest provided one changes to interesting work. There is little real mental fatigue, even after multiplying numbers in one's head all day. Most mental fatigue that we feel results from monotony, disliking the work, and wanting sympathy. Changing the work from time to time should help.

How can you arrange your work so that there are changes to break fatigue?

The day's work is about the most important thing for any of us. Using skills so that the most can be accomplished with the least wear and tear on ourselves is the aim of personal efficiency. One may use his skills in a haphazard sort of a way, as the shiftless Rip van Winkle used his; or he may direct them intelligently. Using skill thus comes to be synonymous with using the skull, or, more precisely, that which lies within the skull.

PERSONAL PROGRESS POINTERS

How can the electric filaments in my rooms be hidden from view?

How can the illumination be made so indirect and diffused that the shadow of my hand on this page is scarcely perceptible?

Does the thermometer indicate that my working surroundings are favorable (68 degrees Fahrenheit)?

Are my work and study rooms evenly illuminated?

What hour tomorrow should I have my eyes examined?

Has too much tobacco or alcohol been a handicap to my progress?

"I am the conqueror of all difficulties."

—the motto of *Honore de Balzac,* French country boy who started to be a lawyer, ended by becoming the greatest novelist of his country. He carried a gold-handled cane with that motto engraved upon it.

Radio, baseball, finance, gardening, and your associates you have studied. In all this have you neglected the most interesting thing of all—yourself? The remainder of this book will introduce you to this most important person. I am certain you will find him a worth-while acquaintance. I know him better than you do just now and can assure you that in spite of his minor faults and shortcomings you will find it most profitable to know him more than casually.

CHAPTER III

PRACTICE, AND SOME OTHER THINGS, MAKE PERFECT

I

BACK in the third grade I filled a page of the copy book with this sentence, "Practice makes perfect." I wrote this particular line twenty-five times; I imagine that altogether I had practice in writing not less than a hundred thousand similar lines before the series of writing books were completed.

That should have been enough practice to have made my writing perfect, but it did not, for the simple reason that practice alone does not make perfect. Practice is only one way — and a very ineffective way at that — of gaining skill, or making perfect.

And what are skills? All animals enter upon life with scores of actions that are entirely unlearned. One does not have to learn to sneeze or to laugh. Just try sneezing when you do not feel like it and see how unsuccessful you are; try laughing when you do not feel like it. It has been estimated that probably 80 per cent of the activities of man are of this unlearned type.

The remaining 20 per cent of the behavior of man is that which determines his position in industry and life. Even though it may comprise no more than one-fifth of his daily behavior, it is by far the most important fifth when one looks to increasing personal efficiency. This one-fifth is the skills.

The moth does not learn to avoid the flame when its wings are singed once, twice, or a dozen times. Our old friend, the cockroach, is not made perfect through practice. It has been found that he can be taught tricks which he will remember for half an hour, but no longer. But men can modify their skills and become more skilled.

Most of this book will be spent in finding out how one can make the most of this one-fifth.

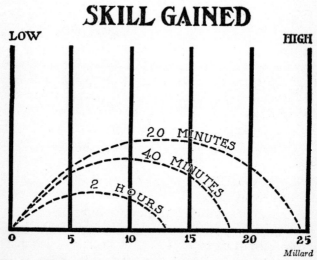

SKILL GAINED

Millard

SKILL IS GAINED BEST WHEN SHORT PERIODS OF PRACTICE ARE USED. PRACTICE FOR SIX TWENTY-MINUTE PERIODS BRINGS TWICE AS MUCH GAIN AS PRACTICE FOR A TWO-HOUR PERIOD, ALTHOUGH THE TOTAL TIME INVESTED IS THE SAME. THE ONE INVESTMENT IS GILT-EDGED.

II

Practice does have something to do with gaining skill, but its value depends largely upon how long one practices.

The lazy man's way has been found to be the best way. Distribute your practice over many short periods; do not practice for a few very long periods. The individual who practices a music lesson for half an hour in the morning and again for half an hour in the afternoon will make more progress than the one who practices for an hour at a time once a day.

When you are learning to drive a car, to typewrite, to play some game of skill, or are memorizing, practice for a short while on many days. You will thus make much better progress. When long periods are used their principal benefit is in furnishing drudgery. They do not develop "will power" — if there is such a thing — and they hamper progress in becoming skilled rather than helping it.

At the time of the Spanish-American War a large concern found itself in great need of moving hundreds of tons of pig iron. The pigs were carried by unskilled laborers, at the rate of about seventeen tons a day.

An efficiency expert came along and told the laborers they were working too hard. He suggested that they work easier, rest more and increase their efficiency with less fatigue. So the foreman blew a whistle at the end of twelve minutes' work, whereupon the laborers laid down their loads of iron and rested for three minutes, when the foreman blew the whistle again as a signal to resume work.

The laborers now spent one-fifth of the time resting. But by doing so they were able to carry forty-five tons a day rather than fifteen tons; their hours were reduced, and their pay increased two-thirds.

By proper rest they had almost tripled their efficiency. By properly spaced rest periods anyone can greatly increase his efficiency. People folding handkerchiefs who work five minutes and then rest one minute do more than those who work steadily. The mental worker who sticks close to his work half an hour and then walks around or, better

[31]

yet, relaxes in his chair and gazes idly out of the window for three minutes, can do more than by working steadily by the half day. And he will be less fatigued at the end of the day.

Do not make your rest intervals too long; that is a waste of time. Do not make them too short; that does not allow greatest efficiency. Experiment with your work until you have found the best ratio of work to rest throughout the day.

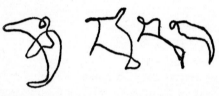

THESE SHOW THE ACTUAL MOVEMENTS OF THE ARM IN OPERATING A DRILL PRESS. FROM LEFT TO RIGHT THEY SHOW HOW ONE WORKER PROGRESSED IN SKILL. SKILL IS GAINED BY ELIMINATING USELESS MOTIONS RATHER THAN BY MAKING FASTER MOTIONS. WHY NOT STUDY BEFORE STARTING TO ELIMINATE USELESS MOTIONS AND ENDEAVORS?

III

Progress in becoming skilled consists largely in *eliminating the useless*.

It was not practice, simply repeating the actions over and over again, that made it possible for the awkward scrawlings of the school boy to become changed into the efficient writing of the executive. The small boy "practicing" penmanship chews his tongue, cranes his neck, rolls his eyes and squirms almost every muscle. After a while he stops rolling his eyes, later he stops squirming his leg muscles. Soon it is possible for him to sit still while writing and he does not grip his pen as though it had wings and was trying to get away from him.

Now he can improve his writing but he must eliminate

more useless movements made by the pen and arm while he is writing. It is not so much practice that improves his penmanship and brings it nearer to perfection as it is using thought to find and select more effective movements.

Stenography is efficiency increasing not because it saves paper — it doesn't — but because it reduces a word of a hundred movements to one or two.

The hardest working woman in our neighborhood is the one who does the least work. This is the exact truth. She is eternally busy from sunrise until long after the sun has set. She does not have a big house to care for, she does not have a number of children to look after. But still she is never caught up with her work.

This woman is a splendid example of one of the great losses in efficiency. She cannot put a dish in the cupboard without making fourteen movements. When she bakes an apple pie, she has to run over two floors to prepare the materials and utensils. Nothing has its place, nothing is organized. She has a kitchen cabinet, but she uses it only as a kitchen table. Apparently she prefers to run around aimlessly rather than work smoothly, quickly, and with the greatest efficiency.

The jazz-band musician is another fellow who would be playing a losing game if he were paid by piece work rather than by the hour.

Many typists are jazzing through their work, having a St. Vitus dance of movements when a few would do. They are doing less work and becoming fatigued faster than if they limited themselves to essentials.

How much of the useless have you eliminated in your work and in your thought? How many steps do you waste in the hurry to catch the car to work because you have not placed your clothes and toilet articles where they can be reached with the least movements? How many useless movements do you make in the course of a day's work because you have the file cases or the dictionary out of reach?

Have you stopped to figure how much more work you could do if your tools were arranged on a shelf over your bench rather than neatly stored in a drawer? Don't waste your time figuring out how much you have lost, give your time to finding out how you can rearrange your desk, or your bench so that the useless is avoided.

Later we shall see how much of the useless there is in your thinking and find out how you can eliminate it.

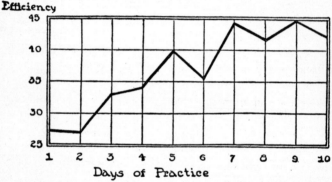

HOW DO WE BECOME SKILLED? THIS CHART SHOWS THAT PROGRESS IS NOT EVEN, SOME DAYS THERE BEING ACTUAL LOSS. INTEREST, PROPER PRACTICE, AND HARD WORK CAN OFTEN AVOID THESE SET-BACKS.

IV

You will acquire skills better if you are active rather than if you are in a position to have someone tell you how to do it. Watching someone while he does what you want to do is a slight aid. You must *do* it. You will learn to drive a car much quicker by shifting gears from the start instead of having some well-meaning instructor put your hands through the movements.

Doing is essential for learning. The doer is the learner.

[34]

If you really want to increase your mental efficiency do these things, do not just read them. Put them to work at the first opportunity.

V

Sometimes, after long periods of practice, there is a marked loss of skill. This is a rather discouraging situation. Some days, progress is rapid; on others, it is just dragging along. There may be an actual loss at certain times.

These periods of no progress are called plateaus, because the chart of accomplishment is flat like a plateau during this period. These plateaus of despond and discouragement are common to all. They may be caused by a temporary slump in interest, or — strange as it may seem — too frequent practice may cause this stalling of progress.

These plateaus are not inevitable. Experimental work has shown that, where one bends his best efforts to overcome this period of no progress, the plateau of despond has given way to progress. Look upon the plateau as a challenge to work all the harder!

A close relative to the plateau is the decreased rate of improvement as the higher levels of skill are neared. The progress is much more rapid and spectacular early in the game, but the finishing touches of the expert are gained after practice which is long and perhaps tedious.

So do not stop because you are slowing up — there is much skill in doing and thinking for you to gain.

VI

Were you ever in a position where you would have given almost anything for an extra hand or finger? Psychology has something to offer you that will be of aid the next time such a situation arises. It will not perform a miracle and grow an additional hand, or even a finger, but it can tell you how to make better use of the hands and fingers you already have. This is to be accomplished by *freeing your hands from their bondage to your eyes.*

The muscles of your body are supplied with two sets of nerves. One set contains motor neurones which stimulate the muscle cells so that they contract and move the bones as desired. The other set is made up of sensory neurones. Every time a muscle moves or is disturbed these sensory neurones are stimulated and carry a message to the brain, informing it of the change in the muscle.

Your eyes do not need to check up the movements of your hands and fingers. Innumerable acts can be performed without any aid from the eyes, and they should be learned that way from the start. Automobile gears can be shifted by the "feel." This "feel" is brought to the brain through the sensory neurones.

Think of the blind man, and still most of us are slaves to our eyes! There is no need to remain in this eternal bondage to your eyes since the muscles have their own eyes in those sensory neurones. The really skilled typist never looks at her fingers or the keyboard. The muscles are self-sufficient; the eyes can be kept free for other uses.

Without the aid of your eyes, take your fountain pen from your pocket, unscrew the cap and place it on the end ready to write. You do not need to take your eyes off this page to do this. Can you tie your necktie without having to watch yourself in the mirror? You should be able to do so.

Would you care for a few extra thoughts, too? Psychology can fulfill this wish also, as we shall discover later.

VII

Cross-training is an expression used by psychologists for the improvement in the use of one limb after the other has been trained in certain movements. If you train your left arm to tap as quickly as possible, your right arm will become a trifle speedier without being put through a period of training. This is cross-training: the right arm profited by the practice of the left.

Cross-training is very limited. It usually carries over for the same identical acts. Training the left arm in quickness will not increase the steadiness of the right. Only the quickness is improved. This cross-training is also limited largely to the same limbs. Training one arm in tapping does not increase the tapping ability of the leg.

VIII

Such a thing as *general training* is largely a myth.

Mathematics and some other school subjects used to be taught, not because of any practical value they might have, but because it was thought that they would develop some imaginary "faculty of reasoning."

Professor E. L. Thorndike recently put this to a test by having students perform problems in algebra and then giving them the same problems a little later using a different set of letters. When the second set of problems was given, it was found that the difficulty had been increased, although there had not been a change in the reasoning involved. The students had been in the *habit* of reasoning with a, b, c, and x, so that when r, w, g, and p, were substituted their reasoning fled.

This explains why the close scientific thinker will go astray in making investments, or why the financier is a poor scientist. Each has got into the habit of reasoning with certain facts; when these are changed, their reasoning is altered.

There is no general training. Train yourself on the

job; Mah Jong trains for Mah Jong, dancing trains for dancing.

If you want skill in invention, don't read the biographies of famous inventors: Invent! If you want skill in managing, manage something, don't play chess!

IX

Skills are formed best when there is some *incentive*. Prizes may be offered to children. Honors, bonuses, and awards of merit may be used as incentives for adults.

The keener the incentive is felt by the individual the better is the skill gained. Faint heart does not win here.

A few years ago a study of the effects of alcohol upon the efficiency of typesetters was started. As soon as the typesetters found that they were under observation, they immediately buckled down to work and did much more than had been thought possible before. For years each man had been working at what appeared to be his best, but as soon as there was some incenitve for them to do better, they did.

Right here we are not interested in what alcohol did to their work. The important fact to remember is that, even when one has apparently reached his highest level of efficiency, it is oftentimes possible to reach still higher levels by a little added effort.

Dr. Frederick W. Taylor, the founder of what is known as scientific management in factories, has said that the average man can do from three to four times as much as he ordinarily does. This can be accomplished without lengthening working hours or driving men so that they are exhausted at the close of the day's work.

The chief limit set to most achievements is one's own efforts. Not all trees grow equally tall and stately, to be sure, and not all men can accomplish the same things.

That is a matter of individual differences. Not all apparent individual differences, however, are *real* differences. Some men just work more earnestly and, as a result, accomplish more than others.

Very few people are doing their most. *Are you?*

X

It is a commonplace that it takes more effort to do something that is displeasing or uninteresting than it would to do the same thing when it is fascinating. If someone could find out a way to make boresome tasks fascinating, he would increase the efficiency of the world several fold.

Let us see what has been done along this line. About 1905, two German psychologists, Ebert and Meumann, made a very careful study of the way memory work was improved by simply "making believe" that it was interesting, even when it was known that it was a long, boresome job. They found that merely deciding to think that the work was going to be interesting improved the work.

More recently Mrs. McCharles, at the University of California, made a more practical study of the influence of attitude on learning than that of Ebert and Meumann. When Mrs. McCharles's subjects pretended that the work ahead of them was going to be interesting and heaps of fun, they learned much more than they had learned with their ordinary attitude or when they thought it was going to be an onerous task.

Perhaps the assumption that the work was going to be interesting really made it interesting, but whether it did or not the fact still stands that they actually learned more and with less effort than when they did not feign their enthusiasm.

This may give some explanation of the apparently marvelous minds of men such as Roosevelt. Everything the Colonel entered into, he took with him his characteristic enthusiasm. Enthusiasm is little more than interest plus energy. Interest itself usually taps all of one's available energy. Faking an interest, whether there is a genuine interest or not, seems to be almost as effective in increasing human efficiency in learning as a genuine enthusiasm.

You can easily verify this yourself.

XI

Rivalry sometimes results in wars. This is one side of the question. It also results in better merchandise, prosperous cities, booming towns, attractive personal appearance. What is of the most importance for us is that rivalry is as effective in urging you on to a higher level of personal efficiency as it is in impelling men to brave the knocks of a football game.

Andrew Carnegie capitalized this fundamental trait of rivalry in bringing his steel mills to a level of production that had been previously considered impossible. He knew how men loved a game, but that in real sport there was always a rival to defeat. In solitaire, it is the "old man"; in golf, it is the "bogie."

This is what Carnegie capitalized. One plant was pitted against another in output; the fuel consumed was on a competitive basis. It was largely this spirit of intense but friendly rivalry that gave the supremacy in the industry to the Carnegie mills.

This contains a valuable suggestion for you. Ambition does not always bring success for it is often a dreamy affair. Some people err in taking others as their rivals; the "old man" you should beat is yesterday's record. Use your rivalry to urge you on to outstrip your old achievements.

Hendrik Willem van Loon

MAY MADNESS: A DIALOGUE ON MARS
What are all those people on earth doing?
They are going!
Where?
Nowhere. Just going!
Whither thou?

(Courtesy The Survey and artist)

Shake hands with your rival! Challenge him to a contest for life!

PERSONAL PROGRESS POINTERS

Have I been practicing so long at a time that I have been unintentionally defeating my personal progress?

Do I use my head to analyze the best way to do things or have I been rushing in, thinking that mere repetition would make me perfect?

Have I been discouraged by my plateaus of no progress, or have these aroused my fighting spirit so that I crashed through these temporary barriers?

Am I a slave to my eyes in dressing and other actions?

Are my desires for character, social usefulness, and self-esteem developed enough to be sufficient incentive for me to make the personal progress I should?

How can I make learning and work as much sport as dancing and bridge?

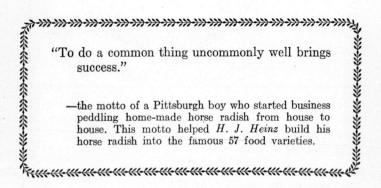

"To do a common thing uncommonly well brings success."

—the motto of a Pittsburgh boy who started business peddling home-made horse radish from house to house. This motto helped *H. J. Heinz* build his horse radish into the famous 57 food varieties.

CHAPTER IV

USING AND ABUSING HABITS

I

You probably use the word "habit" to connote a bad habit. Habit is reserved for such acts as smoking, drinking, and beating one's wife. These are undoubtedly habits, but very unrepresentative ones. Going to church, saying grace before meals, and politeness are also habits. You must stretch your conception of the term to cover these.

When you learn, you are forming habits. Gaining skill is forming habits. If these are not what you think of in connection with habit, the trouble is with your conception and not with the habits.

Some animals are unable to form habits for they cannot learn. Where human beings have the intelligence of an idiot they are unable to form habits; for they, too, are unable to learn.

Habits are a mark of intelligence and not the despicable things that most people think them. That is why I prefer to call them skills. What are commonly called skills are splendid examples of habits. And they are not usually looked upon with contempt. Using habit in the psychological sense, one can as well speak of the skilled drunkard as the habitual drunkard.

Things that we have learned, whether they be operating a typewriter, reading Sanskrit, or identifying tissues under the microscope, are habits. The more we perform them, the more firmly ingrained they become in our nature and the more skillful we become in their use.

Habits are valuable characteristics; they are despicable only when directed in the wrong channels.

Hendrik Willem van Loon

HABITS BOTH:
The soldiers' habits of doing.
The Puritan habits of thinking.
(Courtesy The Survey and artist)

II

There are three kinds of habits psychologically.

First of all there are *habits of doing,* or motor habits. When you absent-mindedly write your name on a blotter, your conduct so far as this act is concerned is dominated by a motor habit. These motor habits, or habits of doing, are all that many people include as habits in their thinking. Ball tossing, typewriting, writing, lacing one's shoes are habits of doing. Such activities, however, do not exhaust all habitual acts.

I have a friend whose specialty is the study of insects.

[44]

He well illustrates that there are habits other than those of doing. I have been with him on walks when his eyes would spy some minute insect on a blade of grass, whereupon he would extract a vial from his pocket and make the unfortunate insect a captive. The important point just at present is not what he did with the insect. The important thing to be remembered is that I could not see the insect until after he had very carefully pointed it out to me.

Our eyes were equally keen, but he would invariably see these insects that I could not until I looked a second or a third time. He had formed certain habits of seeing. *Sensory habits,* such as this one, are fully as important in mental economy as habits of doing. Reading is largely a habit of seeing, a sensory habit. The man who taps the axles on the railway coach has trained his ear to certain sensory habits so that he can detect the least flaw in the axle that might imperil the lives of the passengers.

The third kind of habits, and perhaps the least thought of, was well illustrated a few days ago by an accident I witnessed. A tenderfoot was riding horseback when his mount shied at a strange object along the campus drive. The result was that the rider was thrown and trampled upon.

It was the crowd that gathered which most interested me. The accident attracted a large group of students to the scene. In the course of half an hour, I heard a law student pondering the question whether the rider could secure damages from the man who had rented him a shy mount; within the same half hour, I heard two pre-medical students discussing in a serious way just what physical damage might have been done to the thrown rider; within the same half hour, a girl who is preparing for social service work was heard discussing what should be done for the man's family if he was seriously incapacitated.

[45]

These different ways of thinking about the same event are the result of *habits of thinking*. Different college courses and interests have resulted in different ways of thinking. These ways are habitual. That is why a democrat and a republican have difficulty agreeing upon any political problem: they have formed different habits of thinking.

III

It is not for the psychologist to tell what habits should be formed, but he can emphatically state why we should form as many habits as possible.

The person who can typewrite with the aid of habits of doing can complete a page in fewer minutes than the persons for whom typewriting is not a habit. Habits save time in thought as well as in doing. In composing a business letter, as much advantage is given through habits of thought as is given to typing by habits of doing. *Habits make for economy of time.*

Time is precious! You can save it by turning it over to habit. Habits increase human efficiency by *making it possible to do two things at once.* An habitual act can be performed with but little, if any, thought about it. The muscles can go through their trained motions and sequences guided largely by habit. Thought can be used elsewhere.

Habits should be formed because *they will make you more accurate.* An instructor expects you to produce discords the first time you practice at the piano. Perhaps you know which key to hit but, for some reason or another, the fingers will not act as you want them. The reason the fingers do not go to the right key is that the habit is not formed. After practice has proceeded long enough, the discords will begin to vanish and listeners say, "he is becoming a skilled pianist." The habits have made you more accurate.

Habits should not be left to themselves, but should be carefully selected and as carefully cultivated. Whenever possible you should form habits to increase mental efficiency, but any habit will not serve this purpose. The habits themselves must be such as to further mental and working efficiency.

IV

All habits have grave dangers lurking just around the corner. This is not necessarily because they involve acts that are "bad." It is because of the nature of habits themselves.

Habits make you an "old fogy." Habitual acts and habitual ways of thinking are difficult to change. Unless you know the proper way to break habits, they become tenacious monsters that will bring about stagnation because they offer a front of inertia to change. The person who is in a rut is oftentimes there as the result of habits. They are persistent and he can not lift himself above them.

The way around this difficulty is to *form the habit of changing*, the habit of keeping up with the progress of civilization. Habits can be used to combat habits; they can be used to evade the dangers with which they are pregnant. The progressive person has formed the habit of progressiveness. The "old fogy" has let his old habits with their old-fashioned, inefficient acts and thought carry him on. He has failed to form habits to counteract the inevitable effect of inefficient stagnation.

V

Another great danger that lurks in habits is the *waning of attention during habitual performances*. The engineer who has piloted a train over a certain section of the railroad until blowing the whistle for crossings, applying more steam, or the brakes, at a certain place has become habitual is not the safe engineer to ride behind.

The wrong dose of medicine is frequently administered because of this waning of attention. Most automobile collisions occur with experienced, skilled drivers. Attention was off the road and the machine. Habits were in charge of the driving, while the attention was elsewhere.

I know a physician who took pride in stating that, in his two hundredth operation for removing tonsils, he would be able to perform the operation with his eyes closed. Mere practice alone, so he thought, would make him perfect. He neglected the other factors that make for perfection. He tried to clip his two hundred and first case of tonsilectomy with his eyes shut, but he had to open them and work in earnest to save his patient's life!

Again habits must be combated by habits. Form the habit of giving attention to careful, delicate acts, even though they are so skilled as to be second nature.

Habits are dangerous mainly to the person who does not understand them. Knowledge of their pitfalls enables one to avoid them. You must combat these at their source: *form habits of progressiveness and of giving attention.*

VI

You can form habits easily. They almost form themselves without help. Breaking away from this inclination is the hard task which many times comes to be more important than forming habits.

Professor William James, who was one of the first psychologists at Harvard, wrote the classical treatise on breaking habits. It is not enough just to decide to break a habit, Professor James wrote, "one must *decide wholeheartedly* and *not let a single exception occur* after one has started to break a habit." Habits should be *broken off abruptly,* and not gradually. The dope fiend may have to break off his habit gradually because to deprive his body suddenly of its accustomed drug is more than the organism can withstand. Mental habits should be broken differently. They must be stopped suddenly and for all time.

It is for this reason that smoking three cigars today, two tomorrow, one the next day and so on until at last none are smoked is poor psychology. One should stop now! A single exception may undo reams of good resolutions, not because one is weak-willed, but rather because it is the law of breaking habits.

Breaking habits should be *a pleasant experience.* It is poor psychology to make that unpleasant. Refraining from indulging in a pipe of tobacco, or a favorite dish, or a like pastime should be made as pleasant as possible.

Human beings tend to do and repeat those acts that have brought them a maximum of pleasure. To make stopping a habit painful or unpleasant is going against the grain of human nature. The old exercise of the habits that one wants to break should be unpleasant. But refraining from doing as one has done in the past should be made a delight rather than a punishment.

These three sound maxims for breaking habits may be summed up as follows: (1) decide to break it with every particle of moral courage that you have; (2) do not ease off gradually — stop and stay stopped; (3) make breaking the habit a pleasure, not a punishment.

VII

Habits are much like children. When Johnnie is told to stop whistling in the house, whippings and similar forms of punishment are not so effective as one other simple little procedure would be. Johnnie still whistles occasionally in the house, and is in constant terror that he will be caught off his guard.

The way to get children to stop undesirable acts is not to tell them to stop and let that, plus a few paternal paddlings, end matters. Never deny them; in place of this offer them a substitute action. By following this procedure, a parent will be obeyed with less trouble and fuss, and with better results all around.

In the same manner, do not break off your habits. Instead, *provide some substitute action* that is less harmful. Simply breaking it off by brute force will not accomplish as good results, takes more effort, and the effect may not last as long. All the effort needed to break off habits when no substitute is offered does not develop "will power" or strength of character. It merely makes changing habits harder work and the results less certain.

Do not break your habits, *change them*. To break off smoking without offering any substitute is a poor use of psychology. If you have been in the habit of smoking only after meals, find some other way of passing this time and do not sit inanely wondering how long you will be able to stand it. I know of one man who broke off smoking after meal times by cleansing his teeth. He changed habits, freed himself of an undesirable one and substituted a splendid habit in its place. And, what is even more important, all this was done without any great show of mental effort or backsliding because he had gone about it in a sensible manner.

The habit of reading, taking a walk, singing, or writing letters may be substituted for less desirable habits. This not only has the advantage of being a correct use of psychology but has the added advantage of offering a means of gaining greater efficiency through the formation of useful habits.

PERSONAL PROGRESS POINTERS

What habits would I be better for breaking?
Do I have habits of study, work, progress, agreeableness?
What are some other habits I should form?
Can I substitute these desirable habits for some of those
I should like to break?

"Thine own reproach alone do fear."

—the motto adopted by a Scotch immigrant while
still a bobbin boy in a textile mill. This line from
Robert Burns was adopted as a motto early in life
by *Andrew Carnegie*.

CHAPTER V

I

THE first bona fide newspaper in English made its appearance in 1622, at the time of the Civil War in England. The reception accorded it was at least indifferent if not genuinely hostile. The coffee shops of Merrie England were the places where items had been transmitted by word of mouth previous to the appearance of news print. Witty old Ben Jonson, chief of the Coffee House Mongers, summed up the opposition when he stated that by being printed the matter ceased to be news.

But the opposition seems to have hampered the growth of newspapers and magazines not at all. In the United States alone, the increase from 1861 to 1911 was five fold. Along with this enormous growth in the members of the family has been an even greater growth in the size of each member. The paper of 1622 was a single sheet affair, about the size of a small handbill and printed on one side only. Contrast with this a Sunday edition of a modern paper with its reams of paper.

Has this great increase in reading matter been accompanied by an increase in good reading habits, for reading is a combination of habits of doing, seeing, and thinking? The vast amount of material to be read has encouraged slovenly reading. Perhaps many journalistic productions merit such a perusal. This is where they are doubly vicious

. Hendrik Van Loon

"AS A BEACON IS TO A SHIP
SO IS A BOOK TO MAN!"

(Courtesy The Survey and artist)

in fostering bad reading habits, for habit prevails in reading just as in swearing or typewriting.

II

People read from many and varied motives. The commercial traveler scans the current magazines to pass the time while waiting for his train. The mechanic reads in the evening so that he may qualify for a better position. He does this if he is ambitious and wants to make the most of his native equipment. But if he is well satisfied with his 75 cents an hour, he is more likely to read, as does his commercial friend, whatever is available.

Then there is the student who reads laboriously the pages assigned by his instructors. He does not know exactly why but he tries to read them intelligently. The scholar reads the same pages but much differently. He is in search of some definite bit of information so he scans the pages with expectant interest, but the chances are that he will make almost as blundering an affair of it as does the student.

A blundering affair? Yes, because reading is much more than simply sweeping over page after page with the eye or remembering a bit from here and there. If one is to read at all, he should read in the proper way. Even leisurely reading, the reading in the railway station, or the evening reading at home to pass the time should be done in the correct way. If it is not, pernicious habits of reading are formed which it will be impossible to overcome when one does undertake some serious reading.

Children are taught reading in the public schools, that is, they are taught how to pronounce words and get a little sense out of the printed page. But the teachers fail sadly to teach the pupils how to read correctly. Perhaps that is one reason why so much of adult reading amounts to just sitting. We were not taught real reading when we learned to read, but just a pretext at reading.

III

You should *read with a purpose*, not aimlessly. Select your reading matter, and read it for all that is in it. If you are interested in the radio, read about that. Go out of your way to obtain books and articles on this subject. You will end up much better informed on radio than the majority of your acquaintances. You will also find that reading instead of being a monotonous substitute for something else to do, becomes mighty interesting.

This is the point at which the reading of the average student fails as real reading. His purpose — the teacher has assigned the reading; his interest — he has none in his task but is eager to hurry through it and rush out to play with his fellows.

Can you recall some time in your life when you read with a consuming interest such as you seldom manifest now? As you recall this, you will note that what you read at that time has remained in your mind as nothing else has. Interest is one of the strongest factors that make for fixation in your memory. It is an inexpensive tool and contributes greatly to efficiency in thinking by supplying more materials with which to think.

When one is without interests, there is danger of mental decay. Over fifty per cent of the patients in hospitals with mental diseases have schizophrenia, or dementia præcox as it used to be called. One of the most prominent symptoms of this disorder is a constant apathy. The patients manifest an interest in nothing.

What are your interests in reading? Get some reading interests that are going to be of value to you in getting ahead in your work. Do your present interests qualify?

Get some that do! Take a few moments now to assay your interests and then make an opportunity to secure reliant books at a book store or library.

IV

It may begin to appear that this is not reading we are talking about but reasoning instead. And this is exactly the point. Reading is too commonly confused with merely looking at words and turning the page. That is only a degenerate pastime which passes for reading.

Become active yourself; supplement the thought of the page. Even the best author leaves much unwritten. Even the best writer makes many vague statements and you must endeavor to understand them. Good reading matter should stimulate you so that thinking it over would become inevitable. If you are not stimulated to think as you read, one of two things is at fault: You or the reading matter.

As you read with a definite purpose, you will become better qualified to think it over. You will have more pertinent information and supplementing the thought of the page will come almost naturally. This is but one instance of the way in which these psychological steps in reading are interlocked, the one facilitating the other. If there is an omission of one, all will suffer accordingly. None of them should be overlooked. It may mean a serious deprivation to others.

When two morning papers appear on the same morning, the one claiming that the strike settlement was a distinct victory for labor and the other as staunchly maintaining that it was a triumph for capital, what is the reader to do about it? Look at the words and turn the page? When the same event is so differently interpreted, it becomes apparent that there is more to reading than a blind perusal.

[56]

Political news, battles of the World War, and local society events receive the same biased presentation from paper to paper.

The constant reader of a "family" paper usually has a splendid collection of one-sided conceptions and believes in them steadfastly. Such an attitude is not that of our day and generation. Prejudices, those stone walls of narrow-mindedness, cannot long survive under an impartial reading of all the news sources.

What has been said for newspapers applies as directly to magazines and books. The "Mirrors of Washington," if it had been written by a Democrat, would have reflected differently than the same mirrors from the pen of a Republican. It is your duty as the reader to judge the worth of the statements that you read, and even to question so-called facts at times.

Fiction, too, comes in for the same close scrutiny. Portraying life is commonly supplemented by preaching about life from one angle or another. Preachers leave their charges to write, knowing that they can reach a wider audience and probably bring about more good by using their stories as a sugar coating for a bitter pill of theology. Peace propaganda, arms propaganda, prohibition propaganda, booze propaganda, can all be found subtly disguised as best sellers.

I gained a great deal of insight into the mind of Mr. and Mrs. General Public in Chautauqua work. "What did the lecturer of yesterday talk about?" I would ask a group. And I was informed that he had told a story about Ole Bull and had used the word "guts." That lecturer had failed, inasmuch as his auditors had retained only the most non-essential part of his splendid talk.

Mr. and Mrs. General Public also have equally bad habits in reading. They fail to organize their reading; they retain the non-essentials and overlook the essentials. If you should ever attempt to retain everything you read, you would be hopelessly swamped with remotely relevant material. All parts are not of equal worth. Skim the unimportant; read with a critical eye. Forget the trashy parts; remember the worthwhile.

A book is a work of the printer's art. Marking its pages ruins it. This is from the aesthetic viewpoint. From the psychological point of view, underscoring the important passages and writing notes on the margin is valuable, since it aids in emphasizing the points that should be emphasized. Some of the best readers I know carefully underscore everything they read. They get the essence out of every article or book. All of their acquaintances look with respect upon their information. *They are well read because they read well.*

v

Have you marked this book yet! I want you to because I have asked some questions that you should think over seriously and act upon. Have you? Mark the rest of this chapter and then work over the previous pages in the same way. It will pay.

Put your reading to use. Not only should one read with a purpose, with some objective in mind rather than aimlessly, but having read you should immediately proceed to put it to use. Reading should always be followed by talking; that is one way of assuring yourself that you have read intelligently.

At the close of each section the effective reader pauses and thinks over what he has read. He will note how what he has been perusing can be used *by him* in *his own daily* activities. He may talk aloud to himself or explain and discuss them with his friends. Thus by his reading he profits.

VI

We have retained for the next step in reading the one point which common sense would perhaps make the only point. *Remember what you read.* But do not make this the sole, and do not make it the first, aim.

Memorize what is essential, but do not memorize until you understand. The parrot has memory without understanding. So does the person who reads and repeats parrot-like that "overexpansion is the cause of labor friction." Remembering what you read will be easy after you have selected topics that are of interest to you; after you have organized and selected the important facts; after you have put them to use. Then one can scarcely help remembering. But it is well to make a separate point of retaining what you read.

Experiment has shown that simply wanting to remember increases what is remembered from 20 to 60 per cent. Try to remember what you read. More will be said about this in the following chapter.

VII

Roosevelt's friends tell how rapidly he used to read. An ordinary book lasted him only a few hours. He turned the pages he was reading almost synchronously with the ticks of the clock. "Hasty reading," you say? Yes; but also, efficient reading.

It used to be thought that people read letter by letter. Children were taught to read this way but, if they were normal children, they soon outgrew this instruction. That is not the natural method of reading.

After your eye has mastered the mechanics of reading, it no longer reads letter by letter, or even word by word. With experience, a phrase is read as quickly as a letter.

"Each and every" can be read by the trained eye as quickly as the first letter of the phrase.

The following will illustrate the point. Take out your watch and time yourself in this experiment. You are to read the column below silently, not moving the lips, not pronouncing, reading only to recognize the words. Do not look ahead! Read this paragraph again.

When the second hand of your watch is at 60, turn the page and read down the column of letters as quickly as you can recognize each one. When you have recognized the last one, look at your watch and write down the number of seconds it took you to read these twenty letters.

Go ahead as soon as your second hand points to 60. Do not pronounce; do not say them to yourself. Just read to recognize each line.

w
a
h
n
b
f
p
m
x
c
i
g
d
r
u
s
o
x
t
y

Look at your watch now. Write the time it took you to read on this line: —————————

We shall continue the experiment. Do not look ahead! This time you will read short words as you have read these letters. Time yourself as you did before and do it as quickly as you can. Go ahead as soon as your second hand is at 60.

told
and
guns
day
two
was
son
the
but
for
you
fell
has
our
sat
only
job
able
not
may.

Look at your watch now. Write the time it took you to read on this line: ———— 5 ————

It took you only a second or two longer to read twenty words than it did to read twenty letters. If your reading habits are good, you should not have taken more than 2 seconds longer,—a tenth of a second longer to read a word of three letters than to read a single letter!

Words of ten letters can be read as quickly as words of three letters if you have efficient reading habits. Time yourself as before while you read the following words to yourself as quickly as possible.

performance
broadcast
accomplished
efficiency
government
prosperous
underslung
diamond
conversation
prohibition
automobile
political
northern
journalism
appointment
ceremony
luncheon
permission
thoroughly
reading.

Look at your watch now. Write the time it took you to read on this line: —————————

You should have been able to understand each of these words at a glance. You should be able to read each of the following phrases (Do not look ahead!) as rapidly. Time yourself on these as soon as your watch points to 60.

In the afternoon
of the first day
there were many
who demanded
legal changes.
Each and every one
of the opposition
refused to change
and a deadlock
lasted three days.

At the opening
of the session
on the fourth day
a report
was read
suggesting that
they compromise.
The majority
of the delegates
agreed to this
and took action.

Look at your watch.

Did you read this list in almost the same time that
you did the letters? If not *give more attention to the
meaning when you read.* You do not need to read for
eye exercise. The meaning is the important thing. Get it
just as quickly as you can!

Slow readers have improved greatly in reading by de-
voting ten minutes a day to reading as rapidly as possible.
A solid column of a newspaper is splendid for practice.
Biting one's lips and holding the tongue so that words are
not repeated aids in developing rapid reading. The eyes
are forced to go as rapidly as possible. Only the essential

meaning is noticed. After a few regular ten-minute drills reading proficiency is greatly improved. The habit should be developed and extended to all reading.

VIII

Your eyes probably pause seven to ten times as you read each of these lines. With practice in reading meanings, you should be able to read a line of print in a book with only two pauses. To do this, you will have to read for meanings.

You will also have to stop saying the words you read to yourself. There is a time for talking and a time for reading, but keep talking separate from your reading.

Progress steadily from the left to the right of the line of type in reading. Much reading inefficiency is due to glancing back over what has been read. Avoid this loss due to backward glances.

IX

Do you get tired when reading?

Avoid excessive eye movements. Read for ideas and, at the end of each section, rest your eyes by closing them and recalling the meanings you have just read.

Do not read on trains, cars, or busses. Nor should you look out of the windows. Instead, watch the other passengers and relax. Every minute of complete relaxation while riding can be subtracted from your sleep.

Read only with proper illumination.

Keep the book ten to twelve inches from your eyes. When it is closer, there is a continual strain such as you feel when looking cross-eyed. Near work is straining work for the eyes.

Have you been reading this for the meaning? With not more than two glances at each line?

Have you used the dictionary to look up words whose meanings were not clear?

Have you *tried* to remember it?

Have you closed your eyes and recalled each section as it was read?

Have you thought it over? Now is the time to do it.

PERSONAL PROGRESS POINTERS

What time each day shall I use to practice rapid reading?

Am I reading enough of the sort that will help my personal progress?

With whom will I discuss the things I read?

Do I "read with a pencil" so I can underline and make notes?

Is the illumination favorable for my reading?

TEST YOUR READING SKILL

Do not turn this page yet.

On the following page there is a paragraph which you are to read carefully to get the meaning. You are going to be asked questions on it, so read it to get all the sense you can.

Your speed of reading will also be gauged, so read as rapidly as is consistent with thoroughness.

Have a pencil convenient to use in writing answers after you have read the selection.

Before you start set your watch so the minute hand will be at exactly twelve and the second hand at exactly zero and start reading carefully, but rapidly, at once. When you have finished reading look at your watch and note the minutes and seconds it took you to read.

You may turn this page and go ahead as soon as your watch is set.

LEARNING IN A CAT

By Edwina Abbott Cowan

Wichita, Kansas

For some time I had desired to experiment on an animal under conditions which would permit the application of experimental technique with adequate checks and controls but would still present to the animal nothing unusual or abnormal in either the problem or the environment. When a friend offered her cat as a subject and her home as a laboratory I grasped at the opportunity to satisfy this pet desire. I approached the ideal conditions I had in mind only as nearly as ideals may be approached, but if the cat found it unusual to have a wire wastebasket inverted over her she gave no sign and accepted the condition with complete complacency.

The experiments were carried out in Wichita, Kansas, at the home of Mrs. Paul Hart, to whom I cannot sufficiently express my appreciation of her coöperation. They began on January 6, 1921, and were performed daily, with one exception which will be noted later, until March 11.

The subject was a pure bred yellow Persian female cat named Mitzi. She was six years old and had been with her present mistress since she was two months old. In disposition she never met with anything but kindness and never showed a disposition to be anything but obliging. She was acquainted with me and very friendly toward me for some time before I began the experiments and during their progress she grew fond of me.

The delayed reaction was chosen as the subject of observation and the living room of Mrs. Hart's house afforded us an excellent problem box. A davenport stood under a window in the middle of the north wall. At each end of the south wall was an opening, one leading into the kitchen through the dining room, the other affording a turn and

[70]

landing in the stairway and also leading to the kitchen. Both openings were equidistant, one to the left and one to the right, from the east end of the davenport. In the kitchen the stove stood against the north wall completely out of sight from the living room and there was a spot under the stove which was equidistant from both openings into the kitchen.

LOOK AT YOUR WATCH NOW and write down the minutes and seconds on this line:
_____ *1 ~ 15* _____ *43 sec* _____ *1 : 19*

Now, turn to the next page and answer the questions. Do this at once.

DO NOT READ THE SELECTION A SECOND TIME.
Answer these questions without referring back to the selection:

1. Where does the author live?.... *Wichita Kan.*....

2. Did the cat object to having a wire basket placed over her?.... *No*......

2. How often were the experiments performed?.... *daily*....

4. How many weeks were the experiments continued? .... *8* ......

5. In what year were they performed?.... *1936* X *1921*....

6. What color was the cat?.... *white* *Yellow*....

7. What breed was the cat?.... *Persian*....

8. How old was the cat?......

9. What sex was the cat?.... *Female* ....

10. What was the cat's disposition?.. *good* ....

11. How did the cat "take to" the author? *liked it*....

12. What afforded an excellent problem box?.. *Room*....

13. Where did the davenport stand?.... *North*........

14. Could the kitchen stove be seen from the living room?.... *yes*....

15. On which wall were the two equidistant doors? .... *North & South*....

After you have filled in all the blanks you can, you may turn back to the selection and see how many answers you had right. Do not change any. Now, count all the right answers you had and write the number on this line:

_____

The average college student reads the selection in two minutes, and has fourteen of the questions answered correctly.

Turn directly from here to page 77 until six months after you have first read this chapter.

The test on the next three pages is to be taken six months after you have read and used this chapter in your general reading. It will show you if you have improved.

When you are finally ready for the test on the following pages, read again the directions on page 69 before you turn this page.

In starting the test, as soon as your watch is set, turn this page and start reading.

Meanwhile continue with the reading of Chapter 6.

I myself served as stimulus and carried in my hand the little tin plate from which the cat was in the habit of eating. On the plate when I appeared was one piece of kidney. While the experiments lasted the cat was fed meat only in connection with the experiment. Kidney was always the meat used. My procedure was to appear at one door or the other with the plate in my hand and then walk to the stove in the kitchen, place the pan on the marked spot and then retreat to the porch and close the door through the glass pane of which I observed the entrance of the cat.

If she entered through the correct door, the one at which I had appeared, she went straight to the plate and ate her meat. I then returned to the kitchen, picked her up and carried her back to the living room. If she made a mistake I entered before she got to the meat and took her back. No other form of punishment was used than to deprive her of the meat. Ten tests a day were made.

The procedure in the living room changed as the experiment progressed. On the first day Mrs. Hart sat down on the davenport with the cat in her lap. I merely placed the pan of meat here and there in the living room to accustom the cat to the plan. There was no difficulty about this and the cat came to the plate at once as soon as Mrs. Hart let go of her. I may say here that the ease with which the cat made this association and held to it through varying changes of conditions and delays surprised me and confirmed in me a belief I had previously held that the length of time which is sometimes consumed by an animal in "learning" is not due to the fact that the animal forms a single new association slowly but to the fact that the problem association stands in a relation to the animal's previous associations which human beings would describe as wholly irrelevant. That is to say, the process of forming one new problem association may involve the formation of countless other associations on the part of the animal before the problem association may be made.

On the second day I made a few tests using the plan of appearing at a door and then placing the plate under the stove. When I placed the plate on the floor I called out to Mrs. Hart and she released the cat. The cat chose the correct door each time and we then introduced ten seconds' delay between my disappearance from the door and

[74]

Mrs. Hart's release of the cat. Mrs. Hart held a watch with a second hand and this obviated the necessity of any signal on my part. She also kept the chart and noted the cat's behavior in the living room.

LOOK AT YOUR WATCH NOW and write down the minutes and seconds on this line:

_____

Now, turn at once to the next page and answer the questions. Do this at once. DO NOT READ THE SELECTION AGAIN!

Answer these questions without referring back to the selection:

1. From what did the cat eat?..............
2. What was it fed in the experiments?...............
3. How was the cat observed?........................
4. What happened when the cat entered through the wrong door?...
5. Which was the correct door?....................
6. Did the procedure in the living room change from day to day?...................
7. Did the cat go to the pan of meat as soon as released? ....
8. Where was the cat before it was released?...........
9. Who released the cat?................
10. Where did the cat go when released?..............
11. Where was the pan placed the first day?...........
12. Where was the pan placed the second day?.........
13. How many seconds' delay was introduced the second day?..............
14. Did the cat choose the right door each time?......
15. Who kept the chart of the cat's behavior?..........

After you have filled in all the blanks you can, you may turn back to the selection and see how many answers you had right. Do not change any.

Now, count all the right answers you had and write the number on this line:

————————————

It takes the average college student two minutes and 30 seconds to read this selection. He has 13 questions answered correctly. *Have you improved in your reading?* If not, give it more attention.

CHAPTER VI

TWO DOZEN MEMORY AIDS

I

THE singer stands before a horn and sings into it while a small wax disc records the selection with an exactness that is uncanny. The disc has remembered the voice of the singer, and reproduces it later with remarkable fidelity. This is a form of memory, organic memory.

The man who labors with his hands bears the indelible impress of his past upon them. Calloused and rough, they are mute testimony to the fact that flesh, as well as wax, is modified by past experiences and retains organic changes as evidence.

The tyro sits down to the typewriter. A letter is typed tediously and slowly. A day later, another letter is typed and this time the action is faster and easier. The nervous system has been modified by the previous experience; it has retained the past experiences, enabling the man to profit by them.

It was not the hands that remembered how to use the typewriter; it was not the hands that made improvement through practice possible. It was the something higher up, neither muscle nor bone. It was the little grey engine.

The memory of the little grey engine makes improvement possible. If it did not remember, we would start life as a new person daily, having everything to learn over again only to forget it on the morrow. Sometimes a person is found whose memory has played him exactly such a trick as this. We may become acquainted with some of these cases later.

An office clerk complained to me some time ago that he had a poor memory. I asked him if he gave it as much attention as he did the finish on his automobile. He got the point at once. Do you?

A good memory depends upon two things. One is the sort of a memory with which you were born. Country children appear to have poorer memories than city children; colored children appear to have poorer memories than white children. If one is born with a naturally poor memory, it is likely that he will always have a poor memory.

But, before you decide finally that you have a poor memory, try using it properly. That is the other half of a good memory. There are persons who have serviceable memories although they were born with poor ones. These are the people who have found out how to make the most of their heritage. There are others who were naturally endowed with good memories but who have not found out the most efficient way of using them.

Which class are you in?

Have you tried to make a more efficient use of your memory? Do you know what modern psychology has discovered about the best way of memorizing? It has many practical suggestions for you that will greatly increase your everyday abilities if you will follow them. Regardless of how well your memory serves you, it is capable of better use, unless you are one in a million.

II

Your memory is something like a woman—it must be handled tactfully. Brute force will accomplish nothing.

A lawyer should know how to manage a woman, but

some time ago I met one on a train who was using brute force on his memory. He told me that if he could improve his memory, he would have greater success. And he was memorizing the time table to give his memory exercise. As a psychologist, I knew that such a procedure would not strengthen his memory, any more than the bones in his arm would be strengthened if he should hit them with a sledge hammer.

But to prove to me that his memory was developing, he called off the list of towns between Chicago and New York and their respective distances from New York. I do not know whether he was correct or not, however, because he could *not remember* where he had placed the time table!

The strength of your memory depends upon the way in which you memorize rather than upon how much it is used. What you want to do is to learn the best ways of memorizing. After you have learned these, follow them rigorously until you have them ingrained as habitual ways of memorizing that you use without thought or effort.

Memory itself, probably, cannot be improved. We are limited by our natural gifts, but the ways in which we memorize can be improved. Therein lies the secret.

III

A boy was injured in a fall from a horse when he was five years old. Following this accident, he lost practically all his memories. Only two of the many words he had known could be remembered after the accident.

For many years, he suffered from a very poor memory. This weakness was so embarrassing that certain methods were adopted to make his memories more serviceable. That these were successful has been demonstrated by the fact that this man with a poor memory has since completed a medical course easily and has become a professor at Ohio University.

There are many memory aids but this man used only three. The first aid he used was to give *close attention* to everything that he wanted to remember. Thus, in medical classes, he sat on the edge of his chair and attentively followed every word of the lecturer. When he studied, he trained himself to give closest attention. After graduation, he continued to give close attention to everything he read and heard since this attitude had become habitual.

The second means this man used to improve his memory was to talk and think over to himself what he had read, heard, or seen. By talking over his memories, he was reinforcing them. He kept at this, too, until it became a firmly fixed habit. You should do the same.

The third means he used was to associate everything new with what he had already stored in his memory. When he ran across a new word, he thought of other words like it, of other new words he had learned, and of places in which he could use the new words. In this way, he associated all his memories. You must acquire this habit, too.

By these three methods the young man with the poor memory became an adult with a memory that his acquaintances consider to be unusual, and he has such a serviceable store of information that he has become an intellectual leader.

IV

The man who first said "it is the little things that count," may have wanted to be funny, but he stated a truth of improving memory. The first "little thing" for you to correct is your intention in remembering.

You have read five chapters of this book; what can you remember? Try to remember this phrase: *intention has a lot to do with retention.* Be sure to remember this because it is illustrative of one of the first steps in putting memory on a serviceable basis.

When one tries to remember, his memory works much better than when it is left to drift for itself. It has been found that, when one tries to remember, he does remember 20 per cent better for a few hours. This same little effort improves memory for longer periods of time by as much as 60 per cent.

Apply this every time you run across something that may be useful. When you are introduced to a person say to yourself: "I must try to remember him"; you *will* remember him much better. When you chance upon a bargain in the advertisements say: "I must remember this" and you will save your pennies, and the embarrassment of forgetfulness.

It is not fair to complain of a poor memory until you have really tried to use what you have in the best way. The ability to remember is there. It is up to you to make the most of it.

v

Can you recall the shape of Italy?

Can you recall as accurately the shape of Germany?

You can remember the shape of Italy much better because, when you studied about Italy, its shape was nothing new. It was merely an old-fashioned boot. When you learned this, you had nothing new to remember. What you did was to connect the new notion of the shape of the country with an old idea already in your head.

The secret of your better memory in this case is that

you had memorized the new through the old. This is a very important memory aid to use continually.

When was the Chicago World's Fair? You probably cannot recall. I am going to show you how to connect the new with the old so that you can remember this date easily. This fair was to celebrate the four hundredth anniversary of the discovery of America. Of course you know that America was discovered in 1492. That is an old memory. Four hundred years later makes the Chicago fair in 1892 but, because the buildings were delayed a year, the actual year of the fair was 1893.

Isn't that much easier than repeating 1893 over and over again? It is not only easier; it makes a more lasting memory. And it is not only more lasting. Doesn't it *mean much more* to you now than it would have if you had merely used brute force and memorized 1893 as the date without having the new memories connected with the old ones?

Do you know the German word for dog? It is *hund.* This can be easily remembered by connecting the new with the old in this way: Hund is much like hound, and hound is an old memory of yours. With one stroke such as this, you have a memory of a foreign word that will last some time.

Not every new thing can be so easily connected with old memories. The point for you to follow, however, is to look for any associations you can possibly find. Do not memorize things as being entirely new; refresh your old memories until you run across some connecting link. You will thus make the new easier to remember, and you will also have strengthened your old memories by reviewing them.

How can you remember this memory aid by connecting it with the others we have given?

When and why was the Chicago World's Fair?

VI

At the circus, you saw many people who were strangers to you. Of all these, which ones would you recognize if you were to see them again? Probably the fat woman and the human skeleton.

Let the fat woman teach you something about improving your memory. She was remembered when hundreds were forgotten because you gave her more attention than you did the normal-sized persons. She was unusual and interesting. This caused you to fix your attention upon her and a more vivid impression was made than if she had gained only casual and passing attention.

What did you read in yesterday's paper? You can probably remember only the items that attracted your attention. That is why most readers remember the novelties of the news rather than the more significant events. You will notice, too, that the advertisements you remember were the large ones or the unusual ones.

The unusual house or the loud automobile is remembered better because they arouse our interest. The interesting public speaker is remembered because interest holds attention, and attention increases the vividness of our memories. Interest and the attention it brings makes otherwise ordinary things vivid. The person who has many and strong interests remembers better than the one with only a few, weak ones.

You probably have trouble remembering names because you are embarrassed when introduced and give attention to complexion and clothes rather than to the name. Hereafter whenever you make a new acquaintance invariably make it a special point to remember their name and their face.

Test your interests in this way: what can you remember from the daily paper? Is it mostly sport news? If so, it is because your interests lie there. Is it the theatrical news? If so, there are your interests too. Or is it the really worthwhile things you remember?

Improve your memory by cultivating an interest in everything you read or hear. Maintain this interest through life, and add further to the vividness of your memories by giving attention only to one thing at a time, and by going slowly until you can feel that a vivid impression has been made. Haste makes waste and not vividness.

One vivid impression is remembered better than three ordinary impressions.

WHAT ARE YOUR INTERESTS?

This brief test will demonstrate how your interests compare with those of college students. In front of each name with which you are familiar and about which you could keep up a short conversation place a check mark.

Sports

Walter Camp
Paavo Nurmi
Grantland Rice
Joie Ray
Sir Thomas Lipton
"Chick" Evans
John Weismueller
William T. Tilden, II
K. M. Landis
Aileen Riggin

Literature

Zane Grey
Sherwood Anderson
Amy Lowell
Frank Swinnerton
Willa Cather
Walter de la Mare
Joseph Conrad
George Jean Nathan
Hendrik Willem van Loon
William Lyon Phelps

Entertainment

David Belasco
George Arliss
Eugene O'Neill
von Stroheim
Mary Pickford
David Wark Griffith
George M. Cohan
Henrik Ibsen
George Bernard Shaw
The Second Mrs. Tanqueray

Science

Jean H. C. Fabre
Raymond Pearl
Thomas Hunt Morgan
John B. Watson
Vernon Kellogg
Jacques Loeb
Thomas C. Chamberlain
Albert A. Michelson
Marie Curie
L. H. Bakeland

If you have more than seven check marks on the list of sports you are above the average college student. The average on the list of literature is four, in entertainment four, and science three.

Does this show your interests to be one-sided? Does this show that you can talk about as many different topics as can the average college student?

VII

Do you reinforce your memory? When you want to remember some facts, do you just look at them or do you repeat the figures? Do you write them down and think about them for a while? If you look at them and think: "How interesting, I must remember this," you are improving your memory by this added effort. But you will not have reinforced it.

Reinforce your memories of the news of the day by talking over what you have read at the table. Reinforce your memories of the best markets by talking over the advertisements. Reinforce your memories of the movies you see by talking about them from time to time.

A student of mine recently performed some experiments which revealed that one remembers 15 per cent more a week after memorizing things that are heard as well as seen. This is a simple way for anyone to improve his memory by merely talking over what he has read or heard. Not only will this aid your memory efficiency but it will give you something about which to talk and perhaps change you from a conversational bore into an interesting person to have around.

Among my friends is a physician who is superintendent of a hospital with twelve hundred patients. This is a great

[85]

accomplishment in itself. More important from the psychologist's point of view is the fact that he has a tenacious memory for names. He has told me that at one time he could remember faces but not names.

He reinforced and improved his memory for names by getting each name through his eyes, his ears, his mental pictures, and by writing it. After he had become adept in this, he never forgot a name memorized.

When you are introduced to a stranger and want to remember the name do not just say "how 'de' you." Repeat his name as often as possible. Disregard etiquette and say: "Glad to know you, Jones." Repeating the name as well as hearing it reinforces your memory.

If you have been in the habit of laboriously writing down things you want to remember, you are reinforcing your memories slightly, but stronger memories have been found to result from repeating and talking over the things to be remembered. Try this out yourself by talking over the significant news of the day, then think the same news over tomorrow and you will be surprised how great an improvement you have made.

VIII

Here is an easy test for you to try on your memory: What did you read about in the last section? Can you remember the section before that, and the one before that? If you go back over your reading, in memory, you will note that you have great difficulty in remembering what you have read even six hours ago. It is but little harder to remember what you read six hours ago than it is what you read two weeks ago.

This illustrates an important and very practical law of

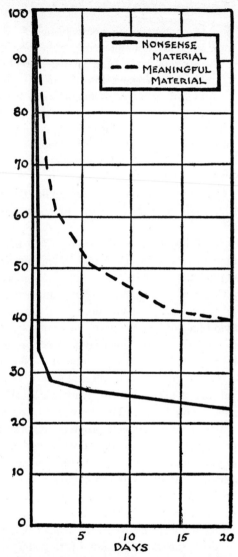

HOW WE FORGET. THE FIRST DAY YOU FORGET
MORE THAN YOU DO IN THE NEXT THIRTY!
THIS CHART SHOWS SOME OTHER VERY PRAC-
TICAL THINGS. WHAT ARE THEY?

memory. For some reason or another, one forgets most rapidly immediately after memorizing. The first day after memorizing one forgets more than he will forget the next thirty days unless he refreshes his memory in the meantime. This rapid fading away of memories is usually disastrous to them.

The principal method to use in order to avoid this rapid loss is to brush up on your memories soon after having memorized. If you have read an interesting article, do not wait until you want to talk about it to revive your memories. The time to revive them and make them permanent is within half a day after the first impression has been made.

If you have children in school, spend some of the time at the evening meal talking over with them the things the teacher taught them during the day. The knowledge retained by the children will be rendered much more useful as well as more permanent if you do.

Take advantage of your spare moments by reviving your recent memories. Whenever you have a minute on your hands, you can turn it to value by offsetting the rapid forgetting of your new memories.

When you are walking recall worthwhile things you have read, seen, and heard. On the car do not read, but devote the time to your personal progress by thinking over your memories. It is easy to day dream, and as easy to dream over your memories. It will take some conscious effort to start the habit of dreaming over — or reinforcing—your memories, but when once started, it is an easy, worthwhile and interesting habit.

Each evening a most profitable half-hour can be spent by thinking over the effectiveness of the happenings of the day. The memories thus systematically revived will change those of iron into steel.

IX

Would you like to have your memories one and a half times as strong as they are now? You can improve them by this amount if you repeat everything you want to remember twice.

How would you like to have your memories twice as strong as they are now? You can more than double their strength if you repeat what you want to remember three times.

Repetition, which is the old stand-by in improving memory, thus is found to be of considerable value, even though there may be diminishing returns. Repetition alone, however, is not the most desirable memory aid. One should understand thoroughly what he is to remember before it is repeated. The layman can memorize difficult medical terms by repeating them alone, but is the memory worth anything if it is not thoroughly understood?

Do not entertain the notion that it is childish to repeat the things you should remember. If you want strong memories you must repeat them. Do not think that your memory is weak if it will not retain things when you read them or mention them only once. You must strengthen your memories by repeating the material you want to remember well. That is the way you memorized the multiplication table, which is probably one of your strongest memories.

When you are introduced repeat the name several times by saying, "Glad to know you, Mr. Jones. We were just talking about the tariff, Mr. Jones." Thus you have repeated the name twice. Jones feels complimented when you mention him by name, and your memories are strengthened every time you do.

If you care to have all your memories as strong as our

AMOUNT LEARNED

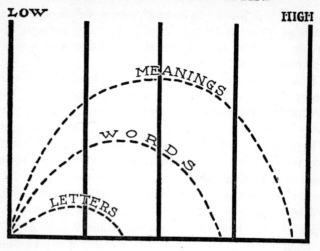

WHEN MEANINGS ARE MEMORIZED PROGRESS IS MOST RAPID

memory of "two times two equals four," use repetition freely.

X

Your sense will improve your memory and your memory in turn will improve your sense, if you go about it in the right way.

One who does not understand the language of finance has a sorry time remembering when he reads the market pages. Likewise, if he is not well versed in sports, a description of a game in the sporting section is scarcely remembered. This is because he does not understand and sense these particular subjects.

A few days ago I was with a group of chemists. The day after, my friend and I talked over the conversation. I remembered but little of it while scarcely a phrase had faded from his memory. I could not remember it because I had not understood what they were talking about. My friend, the chemist, had remembered it because the conversation had made sense for him.

Give your memory an additional lift by memorizing meanings. Can you remember this: Use sense to improve your memory? Can you remember this: Sense memory to your use improve? You remember the one because it has sense for you. The other has the same words but is many times harder to remember because there is no meaning that you can attach to it.

You can remember quicker when you look for the meaning; you will also remember longer when you have memorized the sense. Use the dictionary to help you get clear meanings. If the sense is not clear to you, study over the word or phrase until you understand it. Read your papers and magazines for meanings rather than for words. Look for the meaning in conversations and speeches. You cannot possibly remember all the words of the minister, but you can easily remember the sense of his talk.

Put this into practice now by turning to the editorials and reading one for its meaning. It will put more sense into your head and the sense will make it easier to remember. Try for the next few days to develop the habit of reading for the meanings. Neglect the words for they are important only insofar as they give the meaning.

XI

When does your memory fail you most, in the morning or in the evening? Can you memorize as quickly in the afternoon as in the forenoon?

Last year I experimented with 112 of my students so that I might answer these questions. The experiments lasted six weeks and required almost five thousand tests.

I found that one can memorize for ideas best in the forenoon. It is about 5 per cent less efficient to memorize in the afternoon, and about 6 per cent less efficient to memorize in the evening. From eight until ten in the morning was found to be the best period to memorize for those who arise at seven.

It is probably easiest to memorize in the forenoon because fatigue is least then, and because there are fewer new impressions in the nervous system.

Sunday seems to be the worst day of the week to use one's memory. This is probably because we take things so easily on that day that our mental machinery is not warmed up and working at its best. Early morning memorizing, immediately after rising, is not effective because the mental machinery, as it were, is not warmed up.

If you are doing some serious study, why not rise an hour earlier than usual, exercise a bit to get warmed up, and study then rather than in the evening when efficiency in memory is 6 per cent lower?

Remember that your retentive powers lose in strength gradually from waking to retiring, so do your serious memory work accordingly.

XII

Do you dread memorizing? When you have a name to remember, do you dislike memorizing it? When you have a speech or some shopping items to remember, are you bothered by the fear that you will forget them?

This attitude really makes memorizing harder, and increases your chances of forgetting the very things you want to remember. Your attitude has much to do with your mental efficiency.

At the University of California, it has been found that one's mental efficiency is improved when he *makes believe* that the work he is busy at is fun and not hard. The work itself, of course, cannot be changed, but the efficiency of the mental life in going at the work is greatly increased by making a pleasant approach to it.

You no doubt have seen some one of your acquaintances stand with his heels to the corner and bend over to touch his forefingers at the level of his knees. Now this can be done easily so long as he does not think it is unusually hard or an impossible stunt, but just as soon as there is a crowd around insisting that it is a hard stunt and that it is impossible for him, he finds himself unable to do it. His attitude has made an easy stunt impossible.

It is much the same with memorizing. The child who thinks that the piece he has to learn for Sunday school is hard, will take twice as long to memorize it as he would if he thought it easy. So with your memory; things will be remembered easier and longer if you look upon using your memory as fun rather than as drudgery. No child should be brought up to think that mental work is hard or irksome, and any adult who feels that way should speedily change his attitude.

If you cannot actually and genuinely change your inner attitude, merely "faking" an attitude of pleasure will be of help. Try assuming this attitude that assists your efficiency the first time you note the "drudgery" attitude creeping over you.

After you have fallen into the habit of looking upon memory and all mental work as being great sport, you are likely to find that it is fast becoming a real and permanent attitude. It should.

Why not pretend that work and memorizing and thought are fun?

XIII

Students especially, and all of us to a great extent, seem to think that too much memorizing is bad. In consequence we find the student studying his lessons just barely enough to be able to remember them the following day, and we find the salesman remembering the name of his new customers only a day or two.

Much forgetting is due to the fact that we seem to seek the easiest way and memorize only enough to remember for a few hours or days. Never stop memorizing as soon as you can repeat the name, or date, or information accurately. Spend some additional time memorizing it even after it is apparently well learned.

What can you recall of the Civil War history you were taught in the grades? Probably but little because, at the time, you were, like the rest, studying just barely enough to be able to remember the lesson for the recitation on the following day. Much education is wasted in this way. Education should be a life-long acquisition, but unfortunately it fades rapidly. This is because students are not taught the value of too much memorizing.

Information that is memorized well enough to be remembered tomorrow will not be remembered a week later unless it is overmemorized or other precautions are taken to keep it from fading. After you can remember what you are reading or studying, memorize it a little more. It is this additional memorizing that will make the memory permanent.

The physician who has his information in his head is the one who overmemorized in college; the one who has to consult his books again and again is the one who memorized just enough to get by in his examinations. The engineer who has to use the pocket manual continually is the one who failed to overmemorize.

You can remember certain things you have read in this book today. If you want to remember these tomorrow and make them a part of your permanent information, review them at once and overmemorize them.

Make overmemorizing a habit; it is a "factor of safety."

XIV

Try this memory test and I will tell you whether you are an optimist or a pessimist:

You are to write down as rapidly as you can the names of the first ten persons you think of. You may think of them so rapidly that you will have time to write only their initials. The only restriction is that you think of persons you really know personally. Now, go ahead.

You have written the names of the first ten persons you could remember. Some of these are no doubt persons you dislike in one way or another; others, you may be very fond of. Now write a plus sign in front of all of those you are fond of, and a minus sign in front of the names of all of those whom you dislike.

If you have all plus marks, you are an unusual optimist. On the other hand, if you have four or five minus marks on your list of remembered names, you are probably as pessimistic as anyone I have yet studied. The more disliked names you remembered, the more pessimistic you are.

It is the way the pessimist remembers that makes him gloomy. He has started a vicious circle by remembering more of the unpleasant things and, probably, the more oi them he remembers the more pessimistic he becomes, and the more pessimistic he gets, the more unpleasant things he remembers.

Many psychologists maintain that one remembers pleasant things better than unpleasant ones. If this is true, and it probably is, does the optimist have a better memory than the pessimist?

If you had many minus marks on your list, try changing your attitude and look for pleasant things to remember. Keep this up until it is a firmly established habit.

XV

Would you like to have an imagination such as the inventor or artist or general has? Then cultivate your memory, for it is memory that furnishes the materials for imagination.

Imagination is memory gone wild, or gone to work, depending upon which way you look at it.

When you recall a name or some experience, your memories are passive or static. Can you recall the appearance of the corner house on your block? That is a passive, static memory.

Can you imagine how you would change the appearance of the house if you were to build a sleeping porch or a wing on it? You are still using your memory although most people would speak of it as imagination. But it is still memory. In place of being a passive storehouse, it has now become *active* and has created a new mental experience out of old ones. It is no longer a mere retainer of experiences.

Your memory went wild when you imagined the addition to the house, or your memory was put to work. Advances are made in the world by such a use of memory as this. How can you profit more? Here are some suggestions.

First of all, you must have many memories. Associate every new memory with your old store of memories. That is what imagination is: associating old memories with new ones so that new and efficiency producing combinations are made.

Then you should make it a point to use your memory in a constructive way each day. How would you rearrange the kitchen so as to save steps and make it more convenient? Use your memory actively in answering this problem. Use it again in planning how you would improve the appearance of your yard. Keep on using it constructively and plan a system for relieving traffic congestion.

You cannot have a constructive imagination unless you have a good store of memories and acquire the habit of using them in new ways.

XVI

Memory is famed for the little tricks that it plays on us. We may get some consolation from knowing just how great these tricks may be. When we realize what it might possibly do, the little failures of our everyday existence will not seem so mountainous as they do now.

Newspapers oftentimes carry the report of a person being found wandering around in a city without knowing his name, his past, where he is, or how he happened to be there. These persons are victims of a lapse of memory but, instead of forgetting only a date or a name, they have forgotten all of their past. This disease of memory is known as amnesia.

The amnesia may be for certain periods of the past such as in the case of the young married woman who remembered her maiden name and all of the incidents of her life until the time of her marriage. This is episodic amnesia, in which an episode of one's life is completely, but oftentimes only temporarily, wiped out of memory.

This may give you some comfort the next time you find yourself unable to recall something. Instead of losing just one memory, you might have lost all memory for several years. But, of course, the thing you want to do is to train yourself so thoroughly in proper memorizing that you never lose any worthwhile memory.

About the worst trick one's memory can play is to fizzle out completely. A Pennsylvania clergyman was in an accident a few years ago, after which he lost all his memories, even of the language he had known and of all the objects in the world. He gazed upon trees in amazement for he had no memories of these. Some psychologists worked renewing his lost memory and, within a few years, his memory was restored.

What causes these memory catastrophes? Nobody knows. Sometimes they follow a blow on the head. In other cases, they follow some emotional shock. And, in other cases, they seem to take place spontaneously, the person with amnesia simply waking up after a nap with his past memories gone.

There is a possibility that one can ward off such breakdowns by having his memories stored in the most economical and serviceable form. These lessons may prevent you from waking up with your past a blank if you follow them, and apply them closely.

XVII

Have you ever gone to a strange city and had the peculiar feeling that you had been there before, although you were certain you had not? Have you ever read a news item and had the impression that you remembered reading it before, when you were certain you had not?

These are false memories. There is really no memory but it seems at the time that you can remember the name, the face, the book, the voice, or the incident, although it is the first time you have ever experienced it.

You have probably had a few false memories in your lifetime. Some unfortunate persons get into such a mental condition that everything they experience seems to have been experienced by them some time before.

Many cases of apparent thought reading are nothing but false memories. Two relatives visit and, in the course of the conversation, one relates some incident of a month previous, whereupon the other has a vague feeling that at that time he was dimly aware of the occurrence. Soon this feeling grows until we hear about a case of "genuine" thought transference which, in reality, is nothing more than an example of false memory.

The oriental religious notions that all of us have lived on earth before, but in the form of some animal, perhaps have their foundation in those vague false memories that occur around puberty.

Ghosts that have been "seen" are, in many instances, nothing more than false memories. The person who reports seeing a ghost does not "remember" about it until several weeks afterward, during which time the vague and deceptive feelings develop and soon all the details of the apparition are complete. Of course, in these cases there is no memory at all of the ghost. What has happened, as in all false memories, is that a vague feeling has grown until it actually seems as if the person can remember having been through the experience. There are many causes for persons thinking they see ghosts but this particular cause is for those cases where the individual does not "happen to remember it" until several days, or perhaps a few weeks, have passed.

There is no memory aid that will do away with false memories. All that we can do is to warn you to watch your memories closely, and make certain you do not mistake a false memory for a real memory.

XVIII

Have you ever forgotten an umbrella? Are you in the habit of losing or forgetting your rubbbers? Do you forget some errands and remember others?

You may forget these because you have not gone about

remembering them in the proper way. But, in many cases, one forgets such things as these because he wants to!

The umbrellas, for instance, that people forget are usually decrepit old ones that they are ashamed to carry or perhaps the gift of someone who is now disliked. They really want to forget such equipment and thus avoid embarrassment. The same holds true for rubbers and errands. Errands that one wants to perform and rubbers that one wants to wear are seldom forgotten. Forgetting is a convenient way to get rid of unpleasantness.

A woman does not begin to forget her birthdays until she feels that she is getting older than she would like to be. Likewise, her husband forgets her birthdays when he feels that she is getting old. It is doubtful if a genuinely happy married person will forget wedding anniversaries.

When you have difficulty in recalling someone's name, although you can recall where you met him, it is because you want to forget this particular person. Or, it may be that his name is Smith and, since you would like to forget another person by the name of Smith, the result is that the name becomes a difficult one to remember.

Of course, one does not intentionally try to forget these names. It is the result of a mental trick that is being played by deeper mental currents something like a double personality, or automatic writing, or autosuggestion. But the result is the same. Things that our deeper mental life would like to have us forget are elusive in memory.

The practical application, when one has difficulty in recalling a name or an errand or what not, is to ask oneself, "Why should I want to forget this?" If you have forgotten what the errand was, remind yourself that it was probably something you did not relish doing, and think along this line until you have unearthed it. In doing this, you will not only get a new hold on the lost memory, but you will also find out much about your deeper mental life.

Go back over some of your famous failures of memory and see if you can discover why you wanted to forget.

XIX

How would you like to have a memory like this man:

John S. lives in Iowa. In many ways, he has a most remarkable memory. I have seen him writing down the numbers of all the automobiles that passed his house during the day. Each day he would do this, and he would be able to call off on a moment's notice the numbers of all the automobiles that had passed on any day one mentioned.

He was not bluffing because we had carefully tested him to make certain his phenomenal memorizing was genuine. It took no effort on his part to remember the numbers of a hundred or more automobiles that had passed his residence on a day two years before.

Perhaps you are thinking he was an unusual man. He was. When I knew him, he was a patient in a hospital for the mentally disordered. He could remember all the slight details of such things as numbers with uncanny precision. But he could not remember when to go to meals, or that he had eaten, half an hour after breakfast. The result was that he had to have a person with a less spectacular memory take care of him, to see that he was not rained on and that he remembered to come to meals, and to dress before he went outdoors.

His memory was spectacular, not serviceable. It was not a good memory. The college professor who remembers the exact date and time of day of every minor historical event in ancient history and who forgets where he placed his hat or to put on a collar before going to his classes does not have a good memory. His memory is not serviceable. His consuming interest in ancient history has helped to make his memory one-sided and unserviceable.

Is your memory a good one? Do you remember many insignificant details on some subjects and forget everything on others?

Take yourself in hand and train your memory to take in and retain the worthwhile, important things, and do not try to show off by remembering worthless things such as the number of steps leading to the library or the number of words in a line in this book, or the exact population of the cities of the country, or the age of each congressman.

Memory should be used to gain knowledge and wisdom, not as a storehouse of useless information. The direction for you to follow is to see that you do not remember all the useless information you can. On the contrary, try to remember everything that is worthwhile.

XX

Does your dog know his name? Does he come when you whistle? Does he know what it means when you say "cats!"? If so, he can remember.

Any animal that can be taught tricks, or to obey certain signals, remembers. The farmer's horses remember when they respond to "gee" and "haw." They may not be able to recall their vacation in the pasture or the winter blizzard when they are standing idly in their stalls, but they do remember many things as well as does the farmer's wife who answers the telephone when her particular ring is given.

Birds and fish can be taught tricks. So can the fishworm that they both feed on. Professor R. M. Yerkes has trained ordinary fishworms to follow a certain path to get their food. The fishworm remembered just as surely as you remember the route to the store. Perhaps he could not stay in his burrow and think over the route but, when

he is hungry and turned loose, he will have no difficulty
in finding his food supply in the proper direction.

XXI

Do you have to ask your wife to remind you of errands
and of things to take to work with you? Does she remember anniversary dates while you forget them?

In such instances as these, most men acknowledge that
their wife's memory is superior to theirs. Psychological
tests have shown that there is some basis for this
acknowledgment.

From the time boys and girls first enter school until
they complete their university work, the girls are better
at memory tests. Whether this apparent superiority is
due to the fact that girls work harder at the tests or to
their memory being just naturally better, I do not know.
But, whether the difference is due to their working harder
or not, the result is the same: Men are slightly excelled
by women.

In the elementary grades, the girls are farther ahead
of the boys in the memory tests than they are in college.
In some tests, the girl with the best memory is nine times
ahead of the poorest boy. The average girl, however, is
only slightly ahead of the average boy.

In mechanical or rote memory, there is little difference
between men and women. Men can memorize a long series
of meaningless numbers or letters almost as easily as
women can. Husband and wife, for example, can memorize
these nonsense syllables in about the same time:

nof   rej   wik

But when it comes to memorizing ideas, such as the
thoughts in this article, experiments have shown that the
women do slightly better than the men.

In most mental abilities, the differences between men and women are negligible. The reason why more men than women achieve eminence is probably due to the fact that most women are engaged in home work while men are engaged in work that brings more public fame. Who has ever heard of an eminent housewife? No doubt, if half of the men of the country did housework and half of the women were at work in which it was possible for one to gain eminence, there would be about equal numbers of each sex in positions of prominence.

As it is, the men must give attention to their memories.

XXII

Are you slow to remember?

The old adage of "slow but sure" is wrong psychologically. The slow memorizer is the one whose memory makes the most mistakes and who forgets quickest. The slow memorizer should not justify his slowness by thinking that it means he remembers what he has learned longer than the swift memorizer does.

The thing to do is to try ways of increasing your speed at memorizing. Not by working at it in frantic haste, of course, but by using these memory aids to speed up. If you have been noted as a slow memorizer, it means that you also forget quickly. Do not try to fool yourself on this score. When you hear someone say that he learns slowly but never forgets, you have good grounds for believing that he is wrong in both statements.

Nature seems to have penalized the mental efficiency of the slow person in many ways. The slow reader is the reader who does not understand what he is reading and who soon forgets it. The person who is slow has been found to be poorer in intelligence than the speedy person, even when he is given all the time he wants.

You need not be a slow memorizer. Take your memorizing coolly, but speed it up as much as you can. The slow memorizer has better chances for improving his memory than the speedy one because he is using his memory less efficiently.

XXIII

What happened to the multiplication table that you learned in school? What became of the memories of yesterday's paper? Modern psychologists do not think they have entirely disappeared but have just gone beyond our control.

Thus the Countess of Laval during a delirium spoke in the Breton tongue which she had long since "forgotten." The memories of this language had not entirely disappeared. They had merely gone beyond her voluntary control.

Memory improvement aims to teach how to memorize so that fewer memories will get away from our control. When they do, it is possible, at times, to get the elusive ones back. Thus in dreams, it often happens that what we tried to remember without success during the day suddenly flashes into our head. Again, a daydream will disclose a name or some information that was apparently forgotten but had merely gone beyond control for awhile.

When memory has apparently failed, try rummaging around in a daydream to recover it. Close your eyes and think of scenes connected with the lost memory. If it is a name that has slipped away, mention aloud to yourself names that strike you as being similar to the lost one. Relax your attention and let the naming take care of itself, taking care only to keep it directed toward discovering the lost memory. If this does not recover the "lost" memory, think about it just before going to sleep. You may recover it in a dream or upon awakening.

You have thousands of lost memories. A good way to brush up on them is to have a daydream "stock taking" every day. Do not build castles in Spain during this reverie but recall the odds and ends of information you possess or the educational experiences you have been through. If you can revive these forgotten memories, you will be astonished at the wealth of information you really possess.

XXIV

Is your memory still young or is it getting old? After we see how memory acts as it becomes old, you can answer this important question for yourself.

I spent one Fourth of July in a Home for the Aged. One old woman noticed the flags flying and asked why they were displayed. When she was told that it was Independence Day, she described in detail the guests and dinner she had on the same day forty years before.

Less than fifteen minutes after she had completed her narrative, she was apparently astonished to notice flags flying. She did not remember telling in great detail about her guests for she started all over again.

Before noon she had repeated this story no less than six times!

She could remember in full detail many of the events of forty years previous, while she could not remember what she had talked about fifteen minutes before, or even that it was Independence Day after she had been told six times and had talked about it for half a day.

Her memory had aged along with her body.

As memory grows old its characteristic is to be poor, often extremely poor, for recent events, and to have an uncanny precision for very remote events.

The person with an aging memory is truly in a second childhood, for he remembers little more than the events of childhood.

Is it hopeless? A celebrated Russian astronomer began to have a failing memory for the events of the day, then he began to fail at remembering events of the past week. Soon he was unable to remember for a year, and finally only his childhood memories were left.

But he recovered a youthful memory. Shortly after he could remember only his childhood, he regained the memories of his youth, then of his young manhood, then of middle life, and died with a complete memory — a young memory.

Is your memory aging? Do you find that you can remember old experiences better than recent ones? You must use every memory aid at your command to keep your recent memories strong and youthful.

XXV

Your memory is one of the most fundamental aspects of your mental life. It is memory that gives you the materials with which you think.

Dr. Emil Krapelin, the eminent German psychopathologist, found that alcohol depressed the higher mental processes, regardless of the amount of alcohol consumed. Small doses or drinks as well as large doses hampered the working of the mental processes. Small doses from the start were found to have a bad effect on memory, judgment, and thinking in general.

Rats can tell us something about the effects of alcohol on memory and learning. Many experiments have shown that rats learn more slowly when they have been given alcohol. Trained or trick rats cannot remember their tricks as well when they have been given doses of alcohol.

Rats forget almost as quickly as they learn under the influence of this intoxicant.

It is well to remember that alcohol affects memory in these two ways: It is harder to recall the memories we already possess after taking even a small amount of alcohol; it is also difficult to learn new memories after taking small doses of alcohol.

The talkativeness and general elation experienced after imbibing alcohol should not be confused with an increase in mental efficiency. Alcohol may make one forget his troubles and his responsibilities, but it also helps him forget many other things. The person who feels more efficient after drinking is deceived.

When you want to memorize readily, or when you want to use your old memories, do not mix drinks.

XXVI

Just how much should you reasonably expect from your memory? The most wonderful memory I know of is possessed by a psychologist who at one time had just an ordinary memory.

Everything he reads that touches his science is carefully thought over and re-read. In his reading, he has many boresome tables of data to scan through, but he remembers practically every important figure. I have seen him talking to a group of students about different phases of psychology when it was positively uncanny to listen to him quote experiments and data and even give long quotations from experiments in foreign languages.

At one such informal meeting, an out-of-town psychologist was telling of some experiments that he was planning. The one with the excellent memory told him that another psychologist had reported some similar experiments fifteen years before. He went on to tell just how the experiments were arranged, drew a diagram of the apparatus that was used, and gave the exact data that had been reported. This was an obscure experiment in an unimportant field but everything he read was read to be remembered and every detail of this was retained with minute accuracy, even to the page numbers on which certain remarks had been made.

He did not just *happen* to remember this one experiment; he remembers everything that he sets out to remember in this same precise manner. He lectures to his classes for two hours at a time giving exact figures by the dozen without a single reference to any notes or aids. His head does not contain a storehouse of useless information. He reads and thinks to remember and associates everything he reads with what he already knows about the subject, and rememorizes all the important details. Every memory he has is a useful memory.

It takes hard work for him to keep his memories in prime condition. But it has been worth while and it has given him a position of great eminence in the scientific world.

It takes hard work for anyone to have a really wonderful, and not merely a freak, memory. But it is worth anyone's effort to cultivate a serviceable, efficiency-increasing memory.

"One night in 1886, 'Aida' was being sung at the Rio de Janeiro Opera House. A new conductor had the baton. He showed nervousness; the great house stirred uneasily. He bungled a pianissimo passage; he brought in his strings raggedly. A sinister sibilant flew around the galleries! Hiss-sss-sss! went the fine senoritas, sss-sss-sss! went the fierce senors. Distraught, unmanned, hearing a crooked death in every venomous sound, that new conductor broke his baton over his knee and fled weeping from the house. From his lowly place among the cellos rose up then a young Italian who scuttled to the dais and raised his bow for silence. He did not look at the score; he knew it by heart. So came to fame Arturo Toscanini, now hailed as Italy's greatest conductor."

"His feats of memory have become legend. Never has he been seen to use a score. In his head are over one hundred operas, in addition to an enormous concert repertoire. When the jealous ask, 'Why does he not use a score?' they answer themselves 'Bravado!' It is not bravado. Toscanini is so near sighted that he cannot read a note that is more than half a foot under his nose. Long before his great night in Rio de Janeiro, he scraped his big fiddle with no white sheets propped up before him. 'Where is your music?' asked the conductor one day. 'Under the seat of my trousers,' replied Toscanini."

PERSONAL PROGRESS POINTERS

Do I practice recall in my spare moments?

With whom can I talk over my memories?

Do I "overmemorize" so my memories will be more permanent?

Do I intend to remember or leave it to luck?

Do I connect new impressions with my old memories?

"The whole, the boundless continent is ours."

—the motto adopted by *Charles Frohman* who started life peddling theatrical programs, became one of the world's most powerful theatre magnates. He quoted this motto, from Alexander Pope, to fellow passengers as he went down on the ill-fated Lusitania.

CHAPTER VII

I

A FEW years ago a group of engineers dammed up the Father of Waters near Keokuk, Iowa. For many miles from the site of this dam, electric power that had its source in the vision of the applied scientist is today utilized in homes and factories.

People have fallen into a peculiar error of thought regarding the electricity they receive from the power plants along the Mississippi. You stop off in Carrolton, Illinois, and ask where the power comes from. "The river at Keokuk," you are told. From the river? No. They are mistaken, they do not get their power from the river. The Mississippi had been flowing for centuries without ever having given electric power for lighting houses and cooking meals.

The source of this power that serves people in three states is not the waters that are backed up for miles up the river. The real source is in the human thought that was back of the construction of the dam and power plants.

The river is no more the source of the power than the flash of lightning is the source of the power that illuminates your home.

Human thought! That is where the real source of power — social, economic, industrial, and individual — lies! And you should know how to use this power.

The thunderbolt and the flash of lightning across the

[111]

clouded sky are only manifestations of this power that we use in electricity. Savages had observed these phenomena of nature for generations—and they fell on their faces in fearsome awe and built shrines to the fire god who expressed his wrath with a tongue of fire and a voice that shook the earth's foundations.

Your ancestors saw the lightning flash. They saw it splinter trees and ignite houses and they reflected. Benjamin Franklin raised a kite high into the heavens and, as a result, the lightning flash came to serve man.

The difference between the uncontrolled flash of lightning that darts across the skies and the power that obeys the touch of a button or the snap of a switch is the difference between the savage and the civilized man. It is the difference between blind observation and thought. It is the difference between ordinary man and the thinker.

The difference between what men are and what they might be is the difference forged by THOUGHT.

The electricity you control in your home is an obedient, trustworthy servant. The monster flash across the sky, unforewarned, unpredictable, is a dangerous and feared beauty. The same with thought: controlled, directed thought is an obedient, trustworthy servant; abuse in thought, monstrosities of thought, are to be feared as the flash of lightning.

Man can find some mechanical protection from lightning. With the security of a lightning-rod, he can complacently brave the thunder storm in its fury.

There are no mechanical devices to protect man from pitfalls of thinking. He is still subject to the vicissitudes of his own thinking and the thinking of others.

Thought lightning-rods depend for their efficacy, not upon the guarantee of the maker, but upon the coöperation of the user.

II

Man is sometimes distinguished from the rest of Creation as "the animal that can think." Men and women can think, but what they imagine is thinking often is just wishing. Much of the failure and strife in the world is due to loose and wishful thinking.

The first great leaders in straight thinking were Socrates, Plato, and then Aristotle. Their influence on thinking put ancient Greece way ahead.

But from the fall of the Roman Empire until the Renaissance, from about 500 A.D. to 1500 A.D., superstition replaced straight thinking. Disease and poverty spread, along with superstition and myths. No wonder this long period is called the Dark Ages.

Roger Bacon was the man who let the light of straight thinking into the Dark Ages, and prepared the way for modern civilization. He was a well-to-do young man who favored a life of productive thought to one of idleness. Roger Bacon was an Englishman, but do not mistake him for Francis Bacon, of Queen Elizabeth's court, who was no relative.

After graduating from Oxford, Roger Bacon went to Paris where he earned the degree of doctor of theology. He became a Franciscan monk, so he could devote his life to study and thinking. A constructive fault-finder, who persistently found fault with loose thinking in high places, he touched so many tender spots he was put in prison as a trouble-maker.

In 1265 A.D., Pope Clement IV, who admired Bacon's ideas, managed to have him released from prison, and encouraged him to write books about straight thinking. For three years, Bacon wrote furiously, scarcely pausing to sleep. In these books he emphasized pitfalls which lead to incorrect thinking. These pitfalls he called *idols*, or false gods which mislead thinking.

Human nature is as susceptible to these idols today as it was in the Dark Ages. Modern business blunders and political mistakes are often the result of these idols luring people to false conclusions.

You may remember Thomas A. Edison's favorite quotation, a statement by Sir Joshua Reynolds, "There is no expedient to which a man will not resort to avoid the real labor of thinking." It is easier to allow our thinking to follow the idols, than to work up a mental sweat and do some real thinking of our own.

III

Bacon called attention to the *idols of the tribe*—twisted thinking which originates in human nature itself.

An example is the executive who will not hire a man who smokes a pipe. He says his college roommate was a pipe smoker who was easy-going and lazy. So this executive concluded that all pipe smokers are that way.

Forming conclusions from too few, or from superficial observations, is an idol of the tribe. It is a pitfall for everyone unless he looks for cases which might show the first hunches were wrong. This executive overlooks the many hard-working pipe smokers—Generals Douglas MacArthur and Charles Dawes, for instance.

Eugene C. Grace, chairman of the Bethlehem Steel Co. has said: "If I were to prescribe one process in the training of men which is fundamental to success in any field, it would be thorough training in the habit of accurate observation." Thinking is seldom better than the observations on which it is based. But it is an idol of the tribe to take short-cuts and jump to conclusions on flimsy observations, or to discard observations that are unfavorable to our wishes.

[114]

Hendrik Willem van Loon

FOLLOW THE CROWD,
FOLLOW THE BANNER,
OR THINK?
(Courtesy The Survey and artist)

Self-justification is another idol of the tribe which lures thinking into dark alleys. The man who cheats on his income tax but thinks it is all right "since other people cheat," or "because the tax is unfair in my case," is an example of the self-justification idol at work.

Wishing rather than thinking is another idol of the tribe. Sales-managers sometimes wish instead of thinking when they set up quotas. So do people who think they can make a fortune buying penny stocks or betting on the horses.

Blaming the other fellow is another idol of the tribe that makes for crooked thinking. The boss blames the workman, the workman blames his tools, the tool-room man blames the purchasing agent, like a dog chasing its tail. The alibi artist is a blamer rather than a thinker.

Emotional thinking is another such idol. A man who is in a pessimistic mood won't venture, and when he is in an optimistic mood, he ventures recklessly. Centuries before Roger Bacon, broad-shouldered Plato said: "Emotional people are like men standing on their heads; they see all things the wrong way." Cool off before you conclude. Drop that letter written in the heat of emotion into the wastebasket.

Superficial observations, self-justification, blaming others, and emoting rather than thinking, are idols which beset the thinking of all people—unless they keep on guard against these idols.

IV

Idols of the market place mislead people into catching ideas from others, rather than straight thinking for themselves. Bacon called it the market place, because in his day that was where people met in groups. We catch our thinking from the groups we associate with—it's easier to catch than originate thinking.

The young person who associates with questionable characters will be thinking like a racketeer before he realizes it. People who associate mostly in labor groups think more alike, while those who meet in management groups steadily think more alike, and more in the opposite direction.

The sales group get a one-track habit of thinking that makes the production men and credit department seem like their natural enemies. Technicians and specialists sometimes become so narrow in their thinking that jokesters say the specialist knows so much he lacks common sense.

In contrast, the real leader thinks broadly all around a topic, not catching his ideas from the self-interests of minority groups, and makes sound decisions that last for years. George Washington was able to think through the opposing ideas of the politicians of his day, and blend the best ideas into policies that launched the United States successfully, and which are sound policies to this day.

Associate with many groups, to avoid lop-sided thinking. And think for yourself, without blindly following the group.

v

The *idols of the den* are the thought-limiting influence of the most intimate groups to which we belong—our families, or close circle of friends.

"Father always did it this way," is the excuse of those whose thinking is shackled by the idols of the den. This is the cause of slowness to adopt new methods and machines —it is why Cyrus McCormick had to struggle for eight years to get his first reaper sold.

Sometimes this is described as the dead hands of parents holding back the progress of later generations.

The whole family, or den, tends to think alike. Children are brought up to think as the parents do, or take the consequences. Occasionally a child becomes a rebel, and tries hard to think just the opposite from the rest of the family.

[117]

But this rebel may merely be contrary, not thoughtful, as he takes the other side of every conclusion. The rebel keeps feelings stirred up, but he does not stir up real thinking in his own head—just a concoction of false arguments to prove others wrong.

The cliques to which people belong act as an idol of the den to cause lock-step thinking. Members of the clique think alike, and are prejudiced against opinions and doings of other cliques. The clique may be a friendly group that plays cards together during lunch hour, or the one that works together in the west end of the room, or that goes on hunting trips together. The world is full of cliques which lower the ceiling on straight thinking. As has been said, when all people in a group think alike, nobody is thinking much.

VI

Bacon's *idols of the theatre* are fads in thinking. Hosts of people follow and imitate a popular star, or the popular orator of the day. Thinking—or, lack of thinking—runs in fads, just as there are fads in clothes and games.

William Jennings Bryan, the silver-tongued orator, built a large following of people who thought with him that the free coinage of silver would cure all economic ills. This was an idol of the theatre—the crowd accepted the star's conclusions without testing the logic in his thinking.

Nazi ideas were spread through Europe by mass meetings and theatrical spectacles in which the idol of the theatre took the place of straight thinking. Showmanship and propaganda arouse emotions that lead people to accept conclusions without thinking, thus short-circuiting their reasoning.

Teen-agers are especially vulnerable to this idol. So are grown-ups who have not outgrown teen-age tendencies to

Hendrik Willem van Loon

BOW TO "AUTHORITY"—OR THINK?

(Courtesy The Survey and artist)

follow the popular star or leader-of-the-month. Climbing on the band wagon is usually a sign of muddle-headed thinking.

Those who are over-quick to follow the leader, may be whisking their own thinking back to the Dark Ages. The Roger Bacons, on the other hand, test the logic of the new popular ideas before swallowing them. It is not thinking if you let a plausible oracle lead you around by the nose.

VII

Flimsy thinking causes more trouble than sixteen mules. Flimsy thinking makes *isms* possible, misleading people into following self-seeking opportunists. The fanatic can build a big following because many people do not take the effort to think things out, and soundly, for themselves.

Straight thinking does not come naturally to most of us. It has to be learned. Human beings are animals that can think, but we have to be stimulated to think, and then taught to think logically.

Logic used to be a required course in most colleges. Nowadays, many schools do not even have a course in logic. The use of case problems in business administration and law schools is an attempt to stimulate thinking.

Scientific training includes training in scientific thinking —but sometimes the scientist forgets to avoid the idols when he does some political thinking.

Instructors and job trainers sometimes have a knack for stimulating thinking, and showing students how to test their thinking for pitfalls. Such were the great teachers—the Aristotles, the Roger Bacons, the John Lockes, the Mark Hopkinses, the William Jameses.

Mark Hopkins is honored in the American Hall of Fame for his work in stimulating sound thinking as a teacher.

William James, the physician who made himself Harvard's

first professor of psychology, said he picked up the knack of stimulating thinking during family meals as a youth. His father, a distinguished philosopher, was aware of the idols of stimulating thinking during family meals as a youth. His he used meal time conversation to provoke their individual thinking, and to make that thinking straight as an arrow.

Few of us are lucky enough to have such stimulation and guidance in thinking, either at home or at school. We have to pick up straight thinking for ourselves, or blunder through life.

PERSONAL PROGRESS POINTERS

Am I too much inclined to think as those I am with think?

Do I search for instances to support my notions in place of having a rational attitude of impartiality?

How many times in the past day have I blamed the other fellow?

Do I mingle enough with persons who think differently?

Do I have set notions or am I open minded?

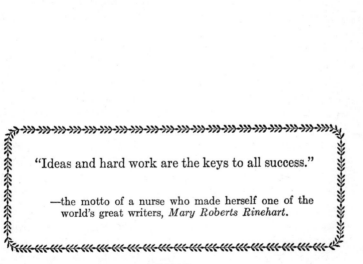

"Ideas and hard work are the keys to all success."

—the motto of a nurse who made herself one of the world's great writers, *Mary Roberts Rinehart.*

CHAPTER VIII

EFFECTIVE THOUGHT

THE executive is in his office behind closed doors. He is not to be interrupted but let us observe him closely for a few moments. Spread out on the desk before him are a few typewritten sheets filled with carefully labelled figures; beside these lies a small map. He says nothing and to all outward appearances he is motionless. The quiet seclusion is pervaded by an atmosphere of solemnity.

Hesitant, and as though undecided, he rings for his stenographer and dictates a long letter, referring frequently to the figures and the map. This letter may make it possible for his business to enter upon an era of great expansion, or it may mean the beginnning of a failure. That all depends.

For more than an hour, this man of business has been alone and quiet. His usual hustle and vim have not been in evidence. He was apparently as motionless as a statue. But was he doing nothing? He was probably doing the hardest work of the week. The man we have just been observing was engaged in active thought.

Now let us turn our observations to another somewhat similar but different scene. Again we find a room in which there is but a single occupant. Comfortably snuggled in an easy chair is a maiden, absorbed in a book. There is no sound except the rustle of each page as it is turned by the eager reader, and the occasional gentle swish of the curtain in the breeze.

Suddenly she drops the book into her lap and rests

her head against the back of the chair. Her eyes are directed through the open window to the beautiful spring landscape. But they see nothing. The spring flowers and the budding trees are not sensed by the maiden. The far-away gaze of her eyes focuses in her mind scenes vastly different. She sees gallant knights and fair ladies. One of the ladies is herself, clothed in the raiment of the Middle Ages. She is just curtseying to a knight in armor when the shrill sound of an automobile signal beneath her window arouses her from the entrancing reverie.

This girl, who had been playing a vigorous game of tennis an hour ago, seems almost like another person. Then she was galloping across the courts and jumping high into the air with all the exuberance of youth to smash a ball close to the net. In strange contrast, we found her in her room, quiet and relaxed. Was she doing nothing? Perhaps accomplishing nothing, but her youthful brain was more active than it ever was over her studies.

She, too, was engaged in thinking, but not in the active, constructive way that we observed in the earlier scene. The maid we have been watching unobserved was enjoying indulgence in passive thinking, for such is daydreaming and the weaving of phantasies. She was accomplishing nothing more than the satisfaction of her wishes for romance. Our business man may have revolutionized his field of industry as the result of his hour of active thinking.

Thinking would appear to be the most active part of our mental life. In thought, we leave the world of our senses we are no longer bound to what we can see or hear or feel A bigger world is opened to us, — the world of ideas. We pass into the realm of things which we know but still cannot touch. Thought is one of the important tools with which we can master our lives.

— and the lives of others.

I

Passive thinking is self-indulgent thinking. It merely imagines obstacles away and does not think of ways to overcome them. It is the kind of thinking that gratifies our wishes in reveries rather than enabling us to overcome the obstacles and actually realize our wishes. Like many of our present-day institutions, it is merely a substitute for the real thing.

Night dreams are a product of passive thinking; daydreams are little more than an extension of night dreaming into our waking life. In neurotic and hysterical patients, this type of thinking predominates. It is also one of the main features of the mental disorder known as schizophrenia or dementia præcox. One-fourth of the 250,000 patients in the mental hospitals of the United States have schizophrenia. They are not the only ones, however, who indulge in passive thinking. They are not the only ones who let passive thinking predominate over active thinking. The neurotics, hysterics and schizophrenics are not aware of the unreality of their daydreams. We call ourselves normal because, even though we indulge in these fanciful heights of daydreaming, we somehow still manage to remember that after all they are only daydreams and not life as it really exists. Otherwise, there is little difference between the passive thinking of the housewife who imagines herself being presented to the Prince of Wales and the unbalanced sailor who thinks he is the Messiah and walks about the wards of the state hospital with a beatific expression, bestowing his blessing upon the other patients.

After you have been rebuked for some mistakes do you find yourself imagining an unanswerable reply you might have given, or imagine that you have suddenly been promoted and have placed your adversary at an irksome task? That is passive thinking. Were you to use the same time

in actively trying to understand your mistake the promotion would come nearer reality.

If I were with you I'd watch for the next occasion when
you get out of difficulties by passive thought. But you must
watch yourself, and you may be certain that soon you
will be caught. Then you will think: "What a silly goose
thing to be thinking that way," laugh to yourself about
yourself, and see that your thoughts get switched back
to actual realities and not things-as-they-might-be, or
things-as-I'd-like-them.

II

Active thinking, in the words of Mr. Dooley, is "thinking that works." We retain mastery over our wishes, we
produce an impression upon the world and we actually
remove or find a way around the obstacles in the way of
our progress. We do not dissipate our mental energies in
fruitless reveries when we employ active thought. And
success is measured by the effects we produce, not by the
dreams we have.

One office clerk after several years' experience saw others
with less experience promoted. Why had he not been?
In active thought he pondered several possibilities. Inac-
curacy? No, because he made fewer mistakes than any
others. Slowness? No. Nor lack of industry or loyalty.
Personality? Perhaps, but he recalled no disagreements
and seemed to get along well with the other employees.
Could it be lack of education? He had only three years
of high school.

Still in active thought he talked his future over with
the head of his department. The clerk found then it was
company policy to promote only high school graduates
to the higher positions. Should he seek another firm;
should he continue a file clerk? He took night school

work for two years, secured his diploma and thus meeting the company policy was promoted.

Another clerk, popular, accurate, rapid, and with only three years' high-school education saw others promoted. Evenings he pondered and imagined he was promoted or had perfected an invention and was living in luxurious ease. His was passive thought.

Most thinking is a strange blending of both of these types. Active thought may be interrupted for a moment by a flash of reverie, or, in reverie, one may chance across, as it were, a thought of sterling worth. And, just as we cannot tell definitely where active thinking leaves off and where the passive begins, neither can one with justified assurance condemn the passive type and praise the active. In many respects, the passive is of more value.

Passive thinking is probably a sort of mental safety valve that functions in maintaining sanity. If one were forced to forego indulgence in night dreams and passive thinking while awake, severe mental disturbances would be dangerously near. The reason for this we shall take up in later chapters. It may be that the ordinary person can let off enough ''mental pressure'' with only night dreams as a safety valve to maintain balance; it may be only the exceptional individual who needs the added safety valve of daydreams. But, until this is known, it may be accepted as not harmful to one's mental balance to have phantasies and to build "castles in Spain" while awake.

In other important respects passive thinking is to be approved. Can you recall the instances in which you have made a brilliant reply to antagonists — in your day-dreams — after the painfully embarrassing episode was past? Can you recall the times when you were ill at ease when trying to recall an elusive name, only to have the fugitive come slipping into your thoughts while you were indulging in a reverie? Can you recall the other times when you have been at a loss to know how to reply to letters when, lo! the happy response came to you in the midst of a daydream? Experiences such as these give some indication of how daydreaming can be put to work to increase mental efficiency. Passive thinking is oftentimes a handicap to efficiency because such contributions as we have mentioned are left to chance. Commonly, no effort is made to put reveries to such purposes as these. Spontaneous contributions are the rule. It becomes our purpose to discover how the few spontaneous eruditions from passive thinking can be transformed into frequent and solicited contributions to mental productivity. For the present, we can do scarcely more than outline some of the first steps to be taken in bringing passive thinking to work for us in the practical affairs of life as well as in unproductive but delectable reveries. Only one ignorant of the findings in psychology within the last score of years would be so foolhardy as to urge the development of active thinking at the annihilation of passive thought.

We find many authenticated records of these usually bizarre and apparently senseless mental states being productive. Such, for instance, is the following incident from the life of Agassiz, the eminent naturalist of the preceding generation: "He had been for two weeks striving to decipher the somewhat obscure impression of a fossil fish on the stone slab in which it was preserved. Weary and perplexed, he put the work aside at last, and tried to dismiss it from his mind. Shortly after, he waked one night persuaded that while asleep he had seen his fish with all the missing features perfectly restored. But, when he tried to hold and make fast the image, it escaped him. Nevertheless, he went early to the Jardin des Plantes, thinking that on looking anew at the impression he should see something which would put him on the track of his vision. In vain — the blurred record was as blank as ever. The next night he saw the fish again, but with no more satisfactory result. When he awoke, it disappeared from his memory as before. Hoping that the same experience might be repeated on the third night, he placed a pencil and paper beside his bed before going to sleep.

"Accordingly, towards morning the fish reappeared in his dream, confusedly at first, but at last with such distinctness that he had no longer any doubt as to its zoological character. Still half dreaming, in perfect darkness, he traced these characters on the sheet of paper at his bedside. In the morning, he was surprised to see in his nocturnal sketch features which he thought it impossible that the fossil itself should reveal. He hastened to the Jardin des Plantes, and, with his drawing as a guide, succeeded in chiselling away the surface of the stone under which portions of the fish proved to be hidden. When wholly exposed it corresponded with his dream and his drawing, and he succeeded in classifying it with ease."

Take your thoughts to bed with you. While undressing think of some problem, then drop it and see what the morning's waking brings.

III

Man has sometimes been distinguished from brutes by being called a thinking animal. It is quite probable, however, that many lower animals are capable of thinking, although it must be admitted that their thinking probably does not approximate the active thinking of which man is capable. The fault to find with man being called a thinking animal is that it places the emphasis in the wrong place. Thinking is not merely an *evidence* of a difference between man and brute that makes man superior; thinking is probably *a cause* of man's superiority. Being able to think has made it possible for man to adapt himself to conditions of life when the brutes would have been exterminated. It is active thinking that has made this possible. The lion trusts blindly in his strength, and the sharpness of his teeth and claws, and the quickness of his paws. Man cannot compete with the lion in these particulars. But man can become active in thinking and devise a bow and arrow, and a spear, or a rifle for which the brute strength and agility of the beast is no match. The lion fights with his paws; man overcomes the lion with his head.

Active thinking takes place usually when there is some need that cannot be met otherwise. Thinking thus enables man to make a better adjustment to life and also makes it possible for him to adjust life to his wants. The brutes cannot do this. The bear builds himself a den in winter and sleeps on a bed of pine needles. Man also builds himself a shelter, but he depends upon the heat from a furnace and not from pine needles. He further provides clothing of a kind that will keep him warm so he will not need to hibernate in his furnace-heated rooms during the colder months.

Evolution has not been a chance affair. Active thinking has been one of the strongest forces in bringing man to his present position of supremacy in the scale of animal life. Active thinking by individuals is the strongest force for giving them supremacy over their life course.

IV

Recall the dinosaur. Can you do so without thinking? You can act without thinking. The boulder that rolls down the mountain side moves, but without thinking. As an insect approaches a human eye, the lids close before one knows it and without thought. Nature has arranged it so that she will take care of such simple actions as this. That is, in most cases she has, but if you go with me to an asylum for the feeble-minded, you will see there idiots whose eyes do not close as some foreign body approaches them.

One can also perform certain well-established habitual actions without being bothered by the need for active thought. No thinking is necessary in dressing — until a collar button is missing.

Many, if not most, actions of daily life are performed without the intervention of active thought. As a matter of fact, in many instances, thought is sometimes a handicap. If the skilled typist begins to think about each key that she pounds in writing the letters, she will have a sorry time of it. When the skilled pianist begins to think about each note, the performance is immediately lowered to mediocrity.

V

You do not need to use active thinking to live and get along from day to day. To form higher habits or to gain better skills, however, it can scarcely be dispensed with. Earthworms and idiots find it easy to live without active thinking. So do too many others.

There are many brain and muscle workers who, when they indulge in active thinking, unhappily direct it into the wrong channels. I feel rather confident that this statement holds for the majority. This is not a matter of psychology; it is just common sense.

Do you spend most of your active thinking in devising more economical and better ways of doing your daily work, or in planning a week-end or evening party? Do you spend as much time in active thought about your own work as you do in finding flaws in the work of others or with the boss? I do not want it to be inferred that I have no sympathy with those who are trying to solve for themselves the problems of labor and society. In many instances, both labor and society would be greatly benefited by directing thought in an active way to the concrete problems of work rather than to an idealistic and semi-passive flight from reality.

Try thinking about things as they are, not as you would like to have them. There is a better chance of having them suit your fancies if you use active thinking about the everyday things of the present.

Of Napoleon it is said: "He never blundered into a victory. He gained his battles in his head before he won them in the field." Of you, what will they say?

VI

Action can take place without thinking, but it is doubtful if thinking can take place without action. By this, I mean more than that all thoughts end in action. Thinking itself is no supernatural power; it is merely one type of action.

An illustration will make this clear. Let us return to the office in which we observed the business man thinking over some commercial campaign. He sat there apparently motionless. His arms hung limply by his side; his head was quiet and poised. Motionless, *apparently*. But let us get closer and watch his lips and throat muscles. Then we shall find that they are not motionless but constantly quivering as though he was talking to himself. If we observe him in especially earnest thought, he may actually whisper to himself.

If we could take this man into the laboratory and set up apparatus that would record the slightest movements of his speech muscles, we should find further that, what we have called thinking, really amounts to talking. That is why modern psychologists are coming to speak of thinking as "sub-vocal speech." It is the same thing as speech but not vocalized. The muscles of speech are as active as in an argument but the breath that vocalized them is absent.

VII

We have seen how thinking may be considered as inaudible speech. The person with many things to talk about audibly is also the person who has many things to think *with,* as well as *about,* inaudibly. Notice this distinction: It is not the rattle-brained person who does a great deal of talking but rather the person with a great deal to talk about.

The tools for active thinking are ideas, especially ideas carried in words. Thinking in terms of language makes thinking definite, not hazy. Words are essentially meanings and not things. Thinking should proceed by meanings and not things. The child starting to school may receive his first exercise in addition when his teacher takes one piece of chalk and places it beside another. The child mind, the undeveloped mind, must think in terms of actual things. A little later, he may be capable of adding one and one but, at first, it is this piece of chalk and this other piece of chalk.

Much adult thinking is after the fashion of this thing and this other thing. It fails in helping development in thought since it is not dealing with meanings but with things.

Enlarge your vocabulary, for a command of words gives command over thoughts. One must have materials with which to think. Get these through the medium of speech, but absorb meanings rather than sounds. If one would do accurate thinking, he must have accurate materials. Do not depend upon hazy, vague notions when your materials for thought can be as accurate as the dictionary makes possible.

A young man complained to me several months ago

about his inability to use words. His vocabulary was so meagre that he felt inferior among college students, and in English he was on the verge of failing because his written work was as simple as his vocabulary. I told him to buy a dictionary. The first thing in the morning he now looks up a *new* word. All the forenoon he uses that word whenever possible. As soon as the noon repast is over he ferrets out another *new* word and uses this one as many times as he can before the day closes. Twice a week he writes home, and uses seven new words in each letter.

Have you ever tried such an exercise? It will be found most interesting and profitable. Search regularly in the dictionary for words, put them to use regularly and keep them in use.

Is your thinking vocabulary as large as your reading vocabulary? Usually it is not. The human failing, when a strange word is met in reading, is either to pass it over or to attempt to get the meaning from the general context of the sentence. Thus a rare opportunity is lost. It results in a one-sided mental development. Words can be read but they cannot be used because they have not been added to our materials for thinking when they should have been. This is one of the reasons why a great gap separates thinking ability from thinking capacity. Make your vocabulary full and rich, not meagre and erroneous. Now is an opportune time to start your dictionary drill.

VIII

Probably one reason why animals cannot approach man in active thinking is to be found in their inability to talk. The donkey has only "hee-haw" with which to think. Animals do not have man's great tools for thought-words. There is a slight possibility that animals may comprehend meanings in some other way than through words; and it is meanings, and not simply words, that are the essential tools for thought.

From time to time, newspapers contain reports of startling cases in which animals seem to be able to talk. A setter dog by the name of Don and owned by a game-warden in Germany is a case in question. Don was a "talking dog" and was supposed to have command of eight German words.

When asked what his name was he replied, "Don." Asked what was the matter with him, he replied, "hunger." When asked what he wanted, he replied with the German word equivalent to something to eat. When shown a cake he said, "cake."

Don startled the world with this eight-word vocabulary. Everyone thought that surely here was a case of a talking dog beyond doubt. But along came some scientist. He found that Don always said his "words" in the same order. If he was asked first what was the matter with him, he replied with his name. Then, asked what his name was, he replied, "Hunger." Shifting the questions brought no change in his responses from their usual order. The result was that all semblance of sense was destroyed in the speech of this talking dog.

And then, of course, what he did say did not closely resemble the words for which they were construed. His word for "hunger," for instance, was "chungue," which resembles hunger only remotely.

Horses and monkeys that reason are also occasionally paraded before the gullible public. Invariably they have been found not to live up to the claims that have been made for them. Not that they were intended intentionally to trick the public, but their trainers along with the general public thought that they were witnessing a genuine manifestation of animal reasoning.

Mathematical horses, perhaps, have been subjected to the closest scientific scrutiny. Such was Clever Hans. Hans could multiply, add, subtract, divide, and manipulate fractions. Hans was told: "I have a number in mind. I subtract nine and have three as a remainder. What is the number?" Whereupon Clever Hans would tap twelve times with his fore foot.

Hans was the most famous horse of all time in this respect. But, after a close examination of his accomplishments, he was found not to be different than any other horse, and other horses cannot multiply, add, and subtract from. It was found that Hans received, unintentionally, of course, certain small signs from his observers that told him when to stop tapping. When Hans started tapping, his trainer, and other observers, leaned slightly forward in expectant interest. When through or to the proper number of taps, his observers naturally straightened back as much as to say, "I told you so." And Clever Hans naturally enough stopped his taps at that point. When he was given a sum to do by shuffling the cards so that the spectators did not know what the correct answer would be, he failed to give the correct number of taps.

IX

Native capacities are the only ones that can be trained and developed. The animals without language cannot develop much thinking ability. They have not been favored in the course of evolution as has man.

Being able to think has brought man to his present position of supremacy, it is not merely a mark of supremacy. Thinking has had a distinct biological value. In conserving thought, one should look for biological value. Thinking, in its stricter sense, we have found to have origin in some need. The need may be real, as for food, or fancied, as for supremacy.

Man commonly meets these needs in thinking by passive thought. That was what the maiden we observed was doing. She was meeting her fancied need for romance in her daydreams. The business man we observed might have met his need of cornering the trade by imagining his reveries so that he had his competitor beaten. But had he done so, he would have found his competitor alert and perhaps far ahead of him when his "Castles in Spain" came tumbling to earth. Passive thinking aids in helping the fittest to survive and to progress only occasionally and accidentally. It is active thinking that separates man from brute; it is active thinking that man should continue to cultivate.

PERSONAL PROGRESS POINTERS

Do I spend more time in active thought than I do in passive thought?

What was the name or fact I could not recall today? If I tried passive thought now I might be able to recall it.

Do I learn and use two new words a day?

Have I used the dictionary for new words I read or hear?

"Yesterday ended last night."

—the favorite motto of *Cyrus H. K. Curtis*, a boy from Maine who started as dry goods clerk, ended as the millionaire publisher of the *Saturday Evening Post* and *Ladies' Home Journal*.

CHAPTER IX

An automobile tourist on his way across the continent got into many embarrassing situations because of his bad temper. When I saw him, he had just smashed his carburetor. As he began to ascend the mountains on the Pacific slope, he was forced to change the gas and air adjustments on account of the higher altitude. Several attempts to do so had met with failure, and his engine was running miserably. In a fit of anger, he had slammed a machinist's hammer into the carburetor.

Throughout the trip, he had been carrying on in a similar manner, so his frightened wife told me. In western Nebraska, he had lost his temper when the jack balked, and he had promptly thrown it into an irrigation ditch beside the road. The automobile had not been to blame for his conduct for his wife said that he had been acting the same way ever since she had known him.

Perhaps you do not have a temper so well developed as this, but from time to time even the most complacent person will become emotionally wrought up over something.

The reason we are all blessed with a temper, although the blessing may not be apparent on the surface, is that it was intended by Nature to be of great usefulness. In most animals, it is still of great usefulness but, when human beings throw away a jack and break a carburetor in a fit of anger, its divine origin seems to be doubtful.

I

Have you ever noticed that an angry person breathes rapidly, clenches his fists, and seems ready to spring at the object that aroused his ire? These bodily changes that accompany anger or fear were given to us by nature to be of great usefulness.

In an intense emotional situation, something happens to our digestive apparatus. Our internal laboratories behave in a fearsome way indeed. If you have been severely frightened or have suffered a bereavement that brought long continued grief, you can testify to poor appetite and digestion. Modern physicians tell us that indigestion, when it is real and not imaginary, is commonly due to emotional causes. Emotional dyspepsia is the most prevalent form of dyspepsia.

A well-fed laboratory cat was placed in front of an X-ray machine so that the experimenters could watch the movements of her stomach while she was digesting food. The stomach was rhythmically contracting and dilating, busily churning the food as any healthy stomach should. The experimenters had a living motion picture of the digestive processes in Tabby.

Then, suddenly, but just as the experimenters had planned, a frisky rat terrier dog was brought into the laboratory and he began to bark at the cat. Naturally enough, this frightened her greatly. Those who were watching the movements of her digestive organs were astonished to notice that immediately those churning or peristaltic movements of the stomach ceased.

The cat had not been harmed by the dog but the fright and fear had caused a serious disturbance. The digestive apparatus had become paralyzed. And it remained paralyzed for some time after the original fear had passed away. It was not until about twenty minutes after the

PULSE·RATE

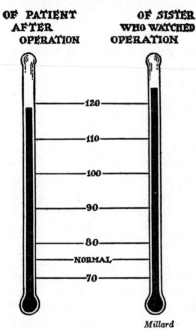

OF PATIENT
AFTER
OPERATION

OF SISTER
WHO WATCHED
OPERATION

120

110

100

90

80

NORMAL

70

Millard

EMOTIONS DISTURB OUR DEEPEST BODILY PROCESSES. AT TIMES THEY
MAY CAUSE MORE DISTURBANCE THAN AN OPERATION

fright that the digestive movements resumed, because emotional disturbances are accompanied by the ejection of a fluid from two little glands, one of which is located on top of each kidney. They are stored away in a protected place, out of sight. They are small glands, but by no means insignificant. A mystery to scientific understanding for ages, these glands have been busy making history for races and nations for generations. They are inaccessible, but they exert an influence over the body that is unmatched by any other behavior of the entire body.

These are the adrenals. They act much the same in you as they do in a cat. All men are possessed of adrenals and, at times, they are possessed by them. Their secretion paralyzes the involuntary muscles. When the dog frightened the cat, the adrenalin paralyzed the muscles of the stomach and intestines bringing digestion to a temporary halt.

This secretion causes the hairs on a cat's back to stand erect when Tabby is frightened or angry. Around the base of these hairs that act so strangely under emotional stress is a little ring of involuntary muscle. As soon as the blood stream brings this secretion known as adrenalin to the involuntary muscles on Tabby's back, it causes the muscles to contract and pull the hairs erect. In human beings, there are no such muscles around the base of hairs, and fear or anger does not make man's hair stand erect. But adrenalin does stop digestion and brings about changes that are of real benefit to the organism.

Adrenalin strengthens the voluntary muscles. It makes them contract quicker and stronger than normally. The adrenalin also provides them with food since it stimulates the liver to liberate the blood sugar that is stored there. This blood sugar is the favorite food of the voluntary muscles. Adrenalin drives the blood from the superficial blood vessels of the skin into the deeper lying arteries and veins. That is why the thoroughly angry person has a face as "white as a sheet." It is another change that is meant to be useful.

What is the usefulness of all this great bodily disturbance? To the ordinary observer, these changes appear to be anything but useful. But the scientist knows that almost everything provided by Nature has been provided for some purpose in the struggle for existence.

Nature is preparing the angry person for some great exertion. Digestion is halted so that all the resources of the body may be directed toward the muscles. The glycogen is sent to the muscles to provide them with a rich food material ready for immediate consumption. The muscles are made to work faster and stronger, and they work with scarcely any fatigue since adrenalin is an antidote for real fatigue. When human beings lived a more primitive existence, these changes were of immense value. They are still of usefulness to animals that must fight for food and, at times, for their lives.

A temper is thus found to be of more use than it would seem to be at first sight. True enough, it does not help us when the jack is thrown away or the foreman is knocked down. But it did have its usefulness at one time. We must learn how to put it to use now.

II

Since civilization has changed considerably, an outbreak of emotion leaves you in a peculiar state. Our soldiers during the Great War offer many examples of this. The prospect of meeting death at almost any moment was not pleasing, especially when there were loved ones across the water. The boys in the trenches were not cowardly, simpering men. They were just human beings in a tight place. The emotional disturbances modified their organism so that they could go over the top with the strength of ten men and bring back a whole nest of enemy snipers.

But their digestion was also hampered. The excitement, the horror, and the dread also caused the gastric juices to slacken up, and the stomach muscles to become partially paralyzed. This resulted in gastric ulcers being a fairly common ailment among the soldiers on foreign soil. Gastric ulcers were much more prevalent among the men in the trenches than among those in the training camps.

It was not the "corn willie" or any of the government provisions that caused these ulcers. It was human nature. It was the bodily changes caused by the emotional excitement among the soldiers.

By the same token, eating with an "emotional" stomach is as bad in civilian life as it is among fighters. A temper has its uses but it has no use before, during, or after meals.

Another effect of the excitement and anxiety of trench warfare has a profound bearing upon the daily conduct of life. The man in the trenches was compelled to be in readiness for fighting at any moment. But still they were cramped into a small space and in an uncomfortable position in spite of the fact that Nature had thrown glycogen into their muscles and the adrenalin had prepared them for heroic exertion.

Did this preparation for action, which was followed by inaction, have any demonstrable effect? Of course it did. Glycogen had been taken to the muscles by the blood stream. When it reached them, it found them already well fed and not prepared to take more nutriment. But the emotional condition prevailed and more glycogen was poured into the blood. This had to be eliminated and caused an overburdening of the kidneys, resulting in glycosuria in which there is an excess of sugar in the body excretions.

Working a temper off thus becomes good advice. Nature

has made preparations for activity. Grouching a fit of anger off does not remove these excess products. If it is left for the organs to do, they become overtaxed.

Keeping a pile of pole wood in the back yard is good mental hygiene. It offers a means of working off a bad disposition and, incidentally, when one looks out of the window, the sight of some probable work may do much toward preventing the occurrence of a tantrum.

III

There is a kindly disposed maiden lady in our neighborhood who offers another illustration of the influence of emotion. For her bravery, she deserves a place beside the soldiers of the Great War. We had not been in the neighborhood more than a few days when the lad of the house started coming home with a cookie in each hand which he said "Miss Elsie" had given him. On the surface, she was a cheerful, happy, undisturbed soul, but underneath this disguised and concealing surface was a veritable ferment of everything exactly the opposite.

The climax of each emotional day was reached, however, when it came time to retire. Then the great struggle ensued. Burglars and midnight prowlers were phantom demons that drove her to agonizing fear nightly. For years she had been suffering, and for years she had been compelled to take a hot-water bottle to bed with her, even in the heat of summer, to warm her chilled feet.

These cold feet were of emotional origin. With the crowding of the blood to the deeper layers of the body, the feet had lost their adequate portion of nature's fuel and the chilling had resulted.

It may be interesting to remark, as we are leaving our old maid friend for the time being, that now she is relieved of her fears. With those of us who worked out with her the groundlessness of her fears, she laughingly jokes about the time when she had cold feet. Now she has her emotions working for her rather than working on her.

One should learn to fear, or hate, or love only when fear or hate or love is needed. When clear thinking is needed, emotions must be subdued. When a good digestion is needed, an emotional state will not bring it.

IV

Anger, fear, and all other emotions are the most energetic mental states. They tap practically the entire reserve of bodily energy. Undirected, they dissipate this reserve; properly directed, they are a source of strength.

The way to control emotions is to put them to work. Do not try to force all of them out of your life. Do not try to drown them out. Do not try to keep from feeling angry or resentful. Let your emotions find expression, but not in their own crude form.

The French psychologist, Ribot, has shown how anger may be put to work and not lead to pugnacity or be penned up dangerously. Righteous indignation is but a form of anger; it is anger put to work. The mean, despicable, crude emotion has been forged, as it were, into noble sentiment.

When you have been tricked by some erstwhile friend do not fly into a tantrum directed against the offender. Try being angry at trickery. Anger on being tricked can be turned into a sentiment of abhorring trickery as neatly as spices and dough can be turned into pastry.

A formula to bear in mind in putting these emotions to work is always to substitute ideals for persons. Never let your refined anger carry over to your neighbor. Let it be an ideal instead. In place of hating people, come to hate them for the fallen or broken ideals they represent. That is a good way to put all emotions to work. Forget

[144]

personalities and think generalities wherever emotions are concerned.

V

Anger means something that very few people think of in connection with an outburst of temper. Anger usually appears to be due to something outside of the person who is angry. It seems as if it were the hammer, or spare tire, or collar button, or almost anything that causes the demonstration of an evil disposition.

These aggravations, serious as they may be, are not the causes of anger. They are only excuses. These pestiferous little articles and events are the innocent bystanders. The real cause of our anger, in practically every instance, is ourselves. It is not the collar button with which we are angry; it is our inability to find it.

This knowledge helps some. One cools off rather quickly when he realizes that his anger, in reality, is directed toward himself. The things that arouse you to anger give much light into your character. It is usually the weak spots that show up plainest when you are angry. Bear this in mind when next anger knocks.

VI

People have been known to commit crimes largely to gain attention. Others have been suspected of feigning ailments for the same reason. All normal human beings appreciate a certain amount of attention and sympathy.

Modern psychology has definitely shown that many apparent invalids are only would-be invalids. There is nothing especially wrong with their bodies, much as they may think that there is. The trouble is located elsewhere. It is in their heads.

Hendrik Willem van Loon

AN OPTIMIST
(Courtesy The Survey and artist)

It is some pernicious idea that is bothering them. Operations, liniment, and baths will not remove the idea! It is mental surgery that they need.

"A fit of blues" is an unintentional but, nevertheless, a genuine effort to gain the sympathy of ourselves and others. Some kink in our nature is greatly satisfied by indulgence in the "blues." Even if we cannot gain the sympathy of others, we can indulge in self pity.

Moods are an indulgence, something like getting drunk. They are emotional sprees that satisfy some deep-lying, and perhaps unknown, craving. But it is there and is nourished to greater growth by each indulgence. If this deep desire cannot be removed by mental surgery, it is profitable to attempt starving it to death.

When moodishly inclined, recall: "it is the joy in misery that is being sought; it is an emotional spree that can be starved to death."

VII

A year old baby was the subject of an experiment at the Johns Hopkins Hospital. The investigators wanted to find out how people come to fear what they do. He was not afraid of birds or animals before the experiment began. When it was over, he was afraid not only of these, but fur coats and fur collars besides.

When rabbits were placed in front of him, he played with them eagerly. He displayed no signs of fear. Then the rabbit was taken away and a loud noise made by striking a steel bar. At once, he was very frightened, threw himself face downward in his bed, and cried.

A few days later, a rabbit was placed on his bed. Ralph reached out to pet the furry creature. Just as his hand came in contact with the fur of the rabbit, one of the experimenters back of Ralph struck the steel bar. The baby did exactly what he had done before when the bar had been sounded — He cried and buried his face in the bed clothes.

And from that time, he was afraid of rabbits!

This shows clearly how one learns to fear what he does. After a few more repetitions of sounding the bar whenever he saw the rabbit, the baby came to be afraid of all animals. Just how far fears of this sort may be acquired is shown by the fact that a few days later, when one of the experimenters, a woman whom Ralph liked, reached toward him in his bed, he drew back in fear because she was wearing a fur coat.

Most people acquire their fears. A person who has been injured in an automobile accident becomes afraid of automobiles. Fear in the presence of fat men may be caused by a fat man having, on one occasion, pulled away the chair in which you were about to sit.

Fears may be unlearned. A sincere effort to get rid of them is the first step. The next step is to go back into the past and determine just when a particular fear started. When fears are once understood, they have been drained of their frightful potency.

Dr. Prince, of Boston, studied the abnormal fears of a woman patient. He used automatic writing to see if some "forgotten" incident might not have been responsible for her anxiety when she saw a cat. An ordinary cat agitated her greatly while a *white cat* nearly threw her into a paroxysm of fear. Dr. Prince tried to get her to recall if at any time she had been harmed by a cat, or to recall any incident of her life that might have given rise to her fear of cats. She was unable to do so. Apparently, if there had been any such experience, it had been "forgotten."

But, with automatic writing, hidden memories were tapped which explained her fears, and also proved that forgotten events are not forgotten but conserved in the deepest part of mental life. Dr. Prince placed a pencil in her hand and, when she was in the proper state, the hand started writing apparently of its own accord. It wrote: "I think I know about the cats. I can now remember myself, a little child playing on the floor with a kitten, and it began to run about the room and had a fit, I think, and it jumped on me, and I was alone and I screamed and called my mother, but no one came, and I was very much frightened. I do not believe I ever told anyone. It was a white kitten. It ran out of the room and, after a bit, I went on playing."

This example is significant for important reasons. It shows how an adult's fears may be traced back to some "forgotten" episode of childhood. The fears may be groundless in the light of adult wisdom but, persisting in the deeper strata of the mental life are "forgotten" childhood memories, that give grounds for the fears.

How can you or I go back over our past or our early childhood, perhaps, to find out how our particular fears and emotional foibles started? Passive thought becomes of use now. If we were to try to do this consciously in a few minutes we might think a solution were found. If one were found so easily — and it probably would not be — the chances are that it would be a false and misleading discovery. By passive thought directed somewhat toward one's fears or tempers some events which have not been thought of for a score of years may be suddenly recalled. A drowsy, easy, imaginative condition facilitates this memory excavating which may unexpectedly disclose the childhood events which cause our emotions to be misdirected.

A "sleepy" evening may often be profitably spent in using passive thought to rummage about in one's forgotten past in search of these emotion-determining events.

VIII

Since most of our emotions are made and not an integral part of our nature, it begins to look encouraging for rebuilding them. Someone has determined that about every seven years each individual is completely rejuvenated, so far as his body is concerned. At the end of seven years, every vestige of the old body cells in the skin, muscles, and bones has been removed by Nature's processes and new ones built to take the place of these worn out ones.

How about our minds? Quite probably they do not change so regularly or so completely. That does not mean that it is impossible to grow a new way of thinking. It is. But it is not done so often as we change our bodies. The reason for this is not far to seek.

The organic processes of Nature change our physical beings automatically. But a change in our habits of thinking demands some *active effort* on our part. Putting a bad temper to work means active effort. It means, first of all, understanding our bad temper, not the temper of the person across the street, but our own, since tempers are built up differently by each individual. That is our reason for laying bare the unpleasant details of a few typical emotional manifestations. Each one has to fill them in with the design and color that are in accordance with his own personal make-up. After this understanding comes the real work — the active energy of putting it to work in its most useful way. Here is where real strength of character shows up.

Human beings are not the only animals that can put their emotions to work. Nearly everyone can remember the household cat and the hunting dog that were on needles and pins when first in the presence of each other. But soon they put their emotions to work — that is, after a few judiciously administered punishments, the lamb and the

MAN HAS BUT ONE ENEMY: HIS OWN FEAR
(Courtesy The Survey and artist)

lion lay down together, came to eat out of the same dish, and quite probably came to like each other immensely. Cats and dogs can do this. How about the climax of creation, man? Can he do it? Can he overcome his emotions and put them to work? He can — but he does not always try. Perhaps, if some one were at hand to punish him for undesirable responses, just as the cat and the dog were punished, he might meet with more success in his efforts.

A good way in which *not* to proceed in putting one's emotions to work is to try bodily repression on the emotions. Simply trying to force them out of your mental life makes matters just that much worse. Forcing something out of your mental life is probably what gives you the emotions you have. Someone has compared this phenomenon to the influence of the moon on the tides. To the observer on this planet, it may appear that only half of the moon is visible. But the other half is there, and is as active in causing the rise and fall of the tides as though it could be seen.

It is much the same with our emotions. Forcing them outside of our mental life does not rid us of them but, on the contrary, they still remain effective, and, like the hidden part of the moon, are still busy pulling our mental tides of emotion.

The woman to whom motherhood has been denied may let her emotions get the best of her and she may cultivate a dislike for children, or she may put her emotions to work by taking up intensive social-service work and mother the families of the slums. The boy who delights in inflicting pain on animals may either let his emotions master him, in which event he will grow up to be a disreputable bully and general ruffian, or he may put these proclivities to work for him and become a successful surgeon.

Then there is the young man who is engaged to be married and getting along only fairly well in his work. When the engagement is suddenly broken, he may let his emotions get the best of him and take to moonshine, or he may put them to work with the result that his colleagues will note that he seems to have fallen in love with his work.

Here is where the value of ideals, and avocations in which a service is rendered, is beginning to become more and more apparent. Services of this sort bring about a release, as it were, of hidden emotional energy. This little smouldering volcano of passion or anger is thus drained off by being put to work. The individual is helped just so much along the road to mental efficiency.

A consuming interest in something through which a living is secured, a consuming interest in some other things that bear the mark of service, and then you will bear the stamp of character — through putting emotions to work.

PERSONAL PROGRESS POINTERS

Do I work off my tempers or grouch them away?

Was I really angry at someone else the last time or was it myself?

Why do I enjoy my moody spells?

There is one strong emotion which bothers me especially, how can I put it to work in building a worthy sentiment?

What can I discover about my bothersome emotions by passive thinking?

"Withal, and in spite of all."

—the motto of a skinny, homely girl with red hair, who was forced to go on the stage against her wishes, by her mother who was unmarried—*Sarah Bernhardt.*

CHAPTER X

PERSONALITY MADE AND REMADE

DURING periods extending over four years, I was in daily contact with thirty-three mentally disordered men. We lived together, ate the same food, attended the same amusements, walked together, and talked together. I came to know these unfortunate men intimately. I knew them better than they understood themselves. If they had really been able to understand themselves, most of them would have been spared a long sojourn in a mental hospital.

I came to like these men with unhealthy minds, and I learned a great deal about myself from them. The better I became acquainted with them, the clearer it became that they were but exaggerations of the personalities one finds among his friends — and, often, in himself.

Among these thirty-three patients was a young man we shall call Charles. He was the most obstinate person I have ever met. If he was told to sit down, he would stand up on a chair. If asked to open his mouth so his throat could be examined, he would seal his lips. Charles did not do this to be intentionally obstinate; he could not help himself. His mental life had gotten the best of him. I sometimes find my mental life trying to play a similar trick when I disagree with someone and search for arguments to justify my attitude.

Then there was a jolly Irish carpenter. He had been a carpenter all his life but, in the hospital, he received wireless messages from Washington and ran the government by return, and just as imaginary, messages. Mike also thought he owned the entire universe. He was content, though he was a great personage, to wash the dishes and sweep the floors. There were others equally interesting and pathetically amusing.

Only one person out of every 150 is insane but, for each person with actual mental disorder, there are dozens with unhealthy personalities. It is from these unhealthy personalities that the mentally disordered develop. Their commonness does not lessen their potent danger.

Forewarned, so the proverb has it, is forearmed. It is well to know about these unhealthy personalities, even though they may turn out to be very personal. A knowledge of them reduces their potency considerably.

I

We perform praiseworthy altruistic acts; we give attention to the comforts of others; we care for the aged and the helpless. But we also contrive to give considerable attention to ourselves.

A balance is usually maintained between the self-centered and the social-centered impulses. In this respect, we live a dual but a balanced existence. This is not a characteristic of an unhealthy personality.

The personality in which this balance is lost is familiar. It is the one in which the self-centered impulses overpower the others. He lives for himself alone; there is no give and take between his personality and others.

These are the *egocentric personalities.*

This name is given them because everything centers about their own interests. Their own ego is the core of their thoughts, plans, and actions.

This personality is scheming. Others must be used for the personal advancement of the egocentric. They are domineering; others must obey their orders and their least desires. They resent being bossed or being forced to take commands.

The egocentric is unfeeling. He will use his friends for his own advantage, and he does not share their misfortune or misery. He excuses his lack of human sympathy by calling it good business, or by saying that his victims would do the same if they had the chance.

If this sounds like a description of some of your friends, or of yourself, do not blame me. If the description is not agreeable, it is because the egocentric personalities are not agreeable. They are neither rare personalities nor are they healthy personalities. By their own one-sidedness, they defeat what they are most desirous of — their own personal progress.

II

Emotional personalities, like the other dangerous personalities, are common and easily discerned when one knows the symptoms and habits. The peculiarities are in the emotions, therefore, the victims are known as *emotional personalities*.

They become greatly excited over events that others take as a matter of course. Life is a long-continued tension for them. There is no calm; everything is hurry and agitation. In these respects, the emotional personalities are typically modern since at present the qualities of hustle and vigor are at a premium. At the same time, their very personalities deny them the full advantage of these qualities. They have excess activity, and lack emotional balance. Other unhealthy personalities are unable to balance their own interests with the interests of others. These personalities are unable to maintain an evenly balanced emotional life within themselves.

From intense anger to the depths of despair is a common

journey for these personalities. They are easily discouraged just as they are easily aroused to a fury. Rebuffs that are not noticed by others become imagined obstacles to the emotional personality. Their greatest obstacle, however, is their own personality.

Their emotional nervousness brings their mental efficiency to still lower levels. They are "fidgety" and easily irritated. A slamming door brings beads of nervous sweat to their brows. A rasping sound or the squeak of a caster sets them on edge and haunts them for a day at a time. An accident, whether seen or merely read about, sends a cold shiver up and down their backs.

Such are the emotional personalities, handicapped by personality — the very thing that brings success to others.

III

Almshouses have to be maintained largely on account of personalities. We work and talk with these same personalities daily, without realizing that they are unhealthy personalities.

The ne'er-do-well personalities have a characteristic inaptitude for work. It almost amounts to laziness. Inadequate might better describe their attitude toward work and life. Accordingly, psychologists have termed these the *inadequate personalities.*

Lack of ambition goes along with their apparent laziness. The inadequate personality is content to live without working or striving for anything better. He is the one who has lived from hand to mouth for thirty years and does not bestir himself at the prospect of facing thirty more years of such inadequate existence. The ambitious person is not inadequate. The person who has accomplished something in the world is not inadequate.

Interest in all things except eating and sleeping is very

Hendrik Willem van Loon

INADEQUATE PERSONALITIES—OR IS SOMETHING ELSE INADEQUATE?
(Courtesy The Survey and artist)

low in these personalities. They have no hobbies to follow with consuming interest after working hours. This lack of interest may be a symptom or a cause of their inadequacy, it is difficult to tell which. At any rate, one of the best antidotes for the inadequate personality is an intense interest in something.

They also seem to be lacking in energy. Great hulks of men with powerful muscles and yet they are unable to carry a board unless someone gives them a lift. They would appear to practice conservation of their bodily resources but, in fact, they lower their resources by not exercising enough to keep fit.

These are unhealthy personalities all around. Almost needless to say, they are not prosperous. After life's middle milestone is passed and their life forces begin to ebb, their more adequate brethren can live on the fruits of a more energetic life. With the approach of old age, the inadequate begins to feel the pinch of his ne'er-do-well traits with which he has been content.

Such personalities are made, not born. The two major ingredients in the prescription for their unmaking are: enthusiasm and a stiff job.

IV

Early one summer morning, I stepped off a train in a small mid-western town. On my way to the hotel I passed the town loafers' rendezvous. In front of a store sat the inadequate personalities of the village. Among them, however, we can be certain was a square-deal personality.

He was dressed in a black broadcloth frock coat, silk hat, fancy vest, loud necktie, and he carried a walking stick. His clothes had evidently been of expensive make and materials, but they now bore unmistakable signs of lack of care. They were soiled, stained, and out of press.

[159]

Hendrik Willem van Loon

THE GREAT-I-AM PERSONALITY

(Courtesy The Survey and artist)

Living with the loafers, this man was strangely in contrast with them.

He had not met with any reverses of fortune that had lowered his estate and had thrown him among the ne'er-do-wells. He had never had an estate to lose or a fortune to be reversed. He was a *paranoid personality.*

He was putting on an impressive appearance; that is one of the characteristics of the paranoid. They think that they are of more importance than they are. Have you ever met such a person?

They might be called square-deal personalities because they frequently complain that they are never getting a square deal. They complain that their employer does not treat them fairly, their landlord is unfair, their neighbors are taking advantage of them, and the foreman is discriminating against them. Have you ever met such an individual?

Sometimes the paranoid imagines that others are persecuting him. The paranoid student maintains that his instructors do not give him the grades he merits. The neighborhood gossip talks spitefully of others oftentimes because she imagines that they are persecuting her.

When you think you are not getting a square deal, think again. Perhaps it is a paranoid personality searching for trouble. When you are much impressed with your own importance and your own accomplishments, think again. Perhaps no one else agrees with you in this particular and certainly others are in a more impartial position to judge; and, when you listen to someone bewailing the unfair treatment that he has received, pause to think of the paranoid personality.

v

Color of hair, tilt of nose, family wealth, and many other things are inherited. There is no justification for blaming a person if his nose tilts up rather than down. This is because of heredity. Inheritence also has a great influence in mental efficiency. Alone, however, it does not account for all the abilities or handicaps of human beings.

Unhealthy personalities are made, not born. I know many people with unhealthy personalities. I also know how these unhealthy personalities came to be made.

Warner is a case in point. He was a college student, one of the brightest on the campus. In grades, he was one of the poorest.

He was conceited, egotistic, scheming, expecting everything from others, and not intending to return the favors given him. He had the type of unhealthy personality that is known as egocentric.

Here is how his personality was made. His parents were uneducated foreigners. He was sensitive about them and their queer manners. As a child, the other children in the neighborhood had not let him play with them. They called him "Greaser" and fought him off every time he ventured out of his alley.

He was a sensitive child and this almost brutal treatment cut deeply. He gradually soothed the hurt by coming to feel that they treated him as they did because they were jealous of some of his superior abilities.

He really felt very inferior. He compensated for this feeling of inferiority by believing that he was in reality much superior to others. His haughty, conceited attitude was not his real, inner attitude. It was a veneer assumed to conceal his real feelings.

Not a single unhealthy personality is the real personality of the individual. They are all spontaneous attempts to cover up a sore spot in memory. We should extend every consideration to these unhealthy personalities. They are the victims of circumstances.

The wrong way to go about remaking an unhealthy

personality is to attempt to force out, as it were, all the unhealthy traits. The traits are but evidences of a deeper-lying cause. It is the cause that must be removed. When the cause has been discovered, then the symptoms commonly fade away.

William had a paranoid personality, until a short time ago. He imagined that he was not being treated fairly by anyone. His fraternity brothers, so he thought, were treating him badly. His instructors were making him do more work than they required of other students and, in return, gave him poorer marks than he deserved. Finally, he began failing in his courses because he refused to do any of the assigned work.

Some of his friends, who knew little of psychology, tried to argue with him and convince him of his error. At that time, he did not know why he reacted as he did and arguments only served to entrench him all the more firmly in his unhealthy personality.

When he was studied psychologically, it was found that he had shown the same traits in high-school and grammar-school work. He had always rebelled at authority and, as soon as one in authority tried to get him to obey, William began to think that this person was persecuting him. His rebellion against authority went back to a time when he was about three years old when his father had whipped him severely. He hated his father; he hated the least resemblance to the parental authority over him.

The reason for his reactions were explained to him and soon his unhealthy personality cleared up. Arguments had helped none; it was not until he had really understood why he was acting in such a manner that his personality began to change for the better.

The remaking of a personality hinges upon a competent understanding of the causes for the personality traits. Get acquainted with your real personality — not the selfish person that others know, but your real self.

VI

To understand fully your own and other personalities, you must know about a mental underworld. Hypnotism brings a mental underworld to light. When a person is hypnotized, it is found that the eyes have been seeing and the mind has kept an accurate record of countless thousands of events and features that the upper world of the mind has never known about.

A young woman was hypnotized by Dr. Morton C. Prince, of Boston, after she had been talking with a man for some time. She was asked to describe the clothes the man wore. She described them in some detail.

Then she was placed in a still deeper hypnosis and the deeper parts of her mental underworld explored to discover if it might not have been possible that she saw more than she had been able to tell about at first. She had. Under deeper hypnosis, she described in detail the stripe in his suit cloth and other minute details of his clothing — and his false teeth!

Her eyes had seen and her mental underworld had accurately recorded details of which her normal self would have been unaware.

Another woman had walked past a certain show-window in a large city. Some time afterwards, she was asked to describe the articles on display there. This she was unable to do. When she had passed the window, she had been looking straight ahead and could only have seen "out of the corner of her eye." How could she have been expected to see and remember anything on display in this window? But she did, when she was hypnotized and her mental

[164]

underworld tapped. In fact, she described faithfully the entire window display!

There is the eye of the subconscious for you! Just as it sees, so it hears, and tastes and feels. Things that we do not sense it senses. Events that we forget, it remembers.

The mental underworld is not selfish. Memory events that it has grasped from our powers of voluntary recollection it gives back but, oftentimes, in such a way that we can not recognize them. It seems as if the subconscious loves a practical joke for it plays multitudes of them on the rest of the mental life.

It really is the best informed part of our mentality for it sees much the rest is blind to, and its ear is far keener than the ear of consciousness. It is a powerful ally and an enemy to be feared especially so since it lives a distinctly separate existence in the case of multiple personalities.

Miss Beauchamp, of Boston, had four personalities that alternated back and forth. These were not exactly unhealthy personalities. They were ordinary personalities like you and three other persons might have, but all in one individual's body.

Part of the time, Miss Beauchamp had a typical old-maidish personality. Then, at other times, all traces of these old-maid characteristics seemed to disappear and, in their place, was an impish rogue personality called Sally. When Sally was the dominating personality, the old maid personality was in the mental underworld. Later, when Sally disappeared for a time, she went down into this same mental underworld.

This mental underworld was within Miss Beauchamp's own mental life. It was a part of her mental life of which she was not aware.

We all have this mental underworld. Usually, however, it is not as well organized as was Miss Beauchamp's. But we have it and it plays as many tricks on us without our being aware of it as Sally played on the old maid.

Alternating personalities are not common. In only a few people does the mental underworld change places with the other parts of their make-up abruptly. More commonly, it breaks through little by little, not spectacularly, but, nevertheless, leaving its impress.

What is inside of your head is really much like an iceberg. Nine-tenths of an iceberg is below the surface of the ocean. Only one-tenth of its vast bulk is visible to the wary mariner. The old sea dog knows this only too well and craftily steers his course well within a zone of safety. Few realize that much more than nine-tenths of the human mind is below the surface. That is why so many fail to steer their course well within a zone of safety. Knowledge is the father of safety and efficiency. The pilot's knowledge of the submerged treachery of the iceberg gives him power to guide his frail craft to security. The knowledge of the submerged trickery of life within one's head, keeps some frail humans from crashing to destruction.

VII

The mental underworld also thinks while we are unaware of this thinking.

Post-hypnotic suggestion shows in an interesting way how the thinking takes places unbeknown to one — in his mental basement, as it were — and later breaks through the barriers and comes upstairs to modify conscious thoughts and actions.

A classical example of this is the young man who was hypnotized. While in this condition, he was told that on the next Friday he would stop at a furniture store and order some baby carriages sent on approval to his betrothed. He was also told to order a gross of nursing bottles sent to the same address.

All this was told him while he was hypnotized, while his mental underworld was on tap and his conscious mental world in temporary oblivion. When he was brought out of the hypnotic condition, he could not consciously remember any command that had been given to him. Did he remember, in his mental underworld, to do what he had been told to do on the coming Friday? Everyone connected with the experiment watched his actions on Friday with consuming interest.

Friday came. He arose, dressed and shaved as usual. Outwardly, he appeared no different than on any other morning. On his way to the office, however, he went a block out of his way. He knew he was doing something unusual and unreasonable, but he could not help himself. The commands that had been given to his mental underworld were controlling his behavior. His mental underworld had remembered what it had been told; it had kept an account of the passage of time. When the stated day arrived, its thoughts broke through the conscious barriers and the man experimented upon did strange things.

He ordered the baby carriages and the nursing bottles! He could not explain why he did, neither could he refrain from ordering them.

The same is true of many of our daily actions. The mental underworld develops ideas of its own; it also acts upon suggestions given in hypnosis. These underworld ideas break through into consciousness and modify our daily thoughts and actions just as surely as they did the conduct of the man who ordered the nursing bottles sent to his fiancée.

The better one understands the tricks that may be played on him by his mental underworld, the better he is prepared to resist domination by this trickster.

VIII

The lazy student has been made energetic by suggestions given him while hypnotized; people with imaginary ailments and foolish fears have had these alleviated by suggestions given them while under the influence of hypnosis.

Of far more interest to us is the fact that one can often be successful in giving himself just such valuable suggestions without having to call in an hypnotist, who might quite likely be a fakir.

You have no doubt noticed how you really seemed to feel in ill-health after several have said that you did not look well. This is a case of suggestion under normal conditions with no hypnosis involved. Have you ever noticed, also, how difficult you find doing something when you have the idea that you will be unable to do it? This is a suggestion of your own working on yourself. In many things can you put suggestions of your own to work in your mental underworld.

In dreams you get a glimpse of your mental underworld attending a Mardi Gras, as it were. While asleep you can be influenced through this channel. Mozart had "The Magic Flute" take form that way; poems and inventions have had just such an origin. Just as you are going to sleep is a most opportune time to give yourself some suggestions. "How shall I reply to that letter?" you may ask yourself after you are in bed and think over the situation until sleep overtakes you. The answer may not come in a dream as did "The Magic Flute" but you will likely be astounded at the ease with which you reply to the letter on the morrow.

Radio operators have had the wireless code taught them while they were sleeping. Others, such as you and I, have not had our mental underworld so educated but have left it to pick up its own education. When our children have habits we think they should not continue we can stand by their bed just as they are going to sleep and say: "To-morrow you are going to have lots of fun playing in our yard. You will play in our own yard and always ask us before you go away." This suggestion can be repeated on different nights and will very likely be effective.

As we use normal suggestion on others while they are sleeping, so can it be used by each of us as we are preparing for sleep. There are three points to follow in using sug-gestion: (1) it is most effective if given when one is drowsy or in a state of abstraction; (2) its effectiveness is increased every time it is repeated; and (3) it should not inadvert-ently suggest the opposite. We did not tell the sleeping child to keep away from the railroad tracks — that would, to some extent, suggest going right there. We did not tell him to keep out of the pantry but rather to stay in the yard. Likewise when you use suggestion on yourself do not say, "I am not going to swear tomorrow," but rather, "Each time I want to give vent to my feelings I'll say 'My word' or 'Cheerio'."

IX

Mental law is back of character traits, lapses of memory, mistakes in speech, the little absent-minded acts of the day. The mental laws bear the name of mental mechan-isms. Certain mental mechanisms are at work in creating the queer traits of the person who thinks his friends are persecuting him. Other mental mechanisms are at work in the person who is polite to the point of obsession. Other mental mechanisms are at work when one forgets to post a letter or keep an appointment. It would seem that most of these are started in our mental underworld, which we must now try to unmask.

If a plank is laid across a brick and one end of the board is stepped on, the opposite end rises in the air. One end

[169]

rises as the other falls. One end compensates for the lowering of the other.

Human beings oftentimes act in a way quite similar to this plank. We shall give some examples to show this. Ways of reacting by *compensation* bear the general name of mental mechanisms. There are many mental mechanisms — compensation is only one of them.

Edward is a student whose predominating mental mechanism seems to be compensation. In high school, he had been fairly popular and active in all school affairs. When he came to college, he expected to be a leader and as popular as he had been in high school. Other boys were pledged to fraternities, but Edward was not approached. He tried to join an honor society but failed. Then he began to feel inferior. Of course he told no one. That was at the bottom of his compensation.

Six months later, the unassuming Edward had changed into a conceited snob. He prided himself upon his intellectual superiority over the other men on the campus. He had what might be called an exaggerated case of the "big head." It was nothing more, however, than a compensation for his inward feeling of inferiority. His mental underworld had played a trick on him. He did not understand himself. He did not realize that all his apparent conceit was nothing but a veil for his inner feeling that was exactly the opposite.

Compensation works out in a multitude of ways. The person who feels his poverty keenly may compensate by taking pride in his honesty. The person who feels inferior because of a weak body may compensate by giving unusual attention to his clothes. The person who is afraid to take part in athletics for fear of being hurt, or who is not in the social swim may compensate by developing into a bookworm who considers book learning and reading the most important things in the world.

[170]

Reformed sinners are often the most ardent and successful evangelists. Their ardor is commonly a compensation for some inward feeling or attitude down in the mental underworld.

X

A common trick played on us by our mental underworld is that of accusing others of doing our thinking. This is not the exact form in which we usually know it, but this is exactly what it is psychologically.

Some time ago I learned about a widow in a small town who accused her neighbors of talking about her. She thought that they were saying mean and despicable things about her. She seemed to be most agitated, however, about their saying that she was a "designing widow."

Inquiry around the neighborhood disclosed that no one was talking about her, at least not in the way she had imagined they were. Her ideas in the matter were entirely unwarranted and for awhile they seemed to be signs of a disordered mind. Disordered minds are normal minds that have become out of order, or exaggerated in their workings. Such was the case with this widow. Many of us are in mental straits similar to this from time to time. It is a test of a well-adjusted mind to be able to adapt itself to situations such as these.

Psychological investigation of this woman disclosed some unexpected mental mechanisms. It was found that these things she was accusing others of saying about her were really things she would like to do. When she imagined they were calling her a designing widow, she was accusing them of the very thing that she was thinking. It was an attempt to avoid facing her own thoughts frankly.

In psychological terms, she was *projecting* her thoughts into the conversation of others. This is the mental mechanism of projection.

[171]

When an individual hears a group of people engaged in conversation in a low tone and imagines that they are talking about him, it is another case of projection.

The social reformer is often fighting what is really strongest within himself rather than in society. The student who thinks his instructors are set against him is really accusing them of something that is within his own mental life. The voice of conscience is not a projection, but it may be projected into the thoughts of others.

The gossip, as she spreads scandal about others, is usually accusing others of having done what she would like to do. Her deeper mental life has played a trick on her. What she is accusing others of really expresses her own nature.

XI

Why do you prefer a four-in-hand tie to a bow tie? You probably can assign some plausible reason for this preference. This is not a reason, however, it is an excuse, or what is known psychologically as a *rationalization*.

A few weeks ago I talked with a student whose conversation for several hours was little more than a series of these excuses. He called them arguments and reasons but they were not. They were nothing but excuses or rationalizations. He argued for a long time that nothing but books should count in college. Dances, parties, athletics, and all similar outside activities, so he *apparently* reasoned, should be abolished from the school.

I listened patiently to his words. Then I asked him how he had liked his high-school friends. Soon, he was telling me about some of the dances and escapades he was a party to back in his high-school days only a few years previously. He was evidently sincere when he said that he had been popular among the high-school students.

Then I followed up my psychological attack on him. I

asked him if he had expected to continue to be just as popular when he came to college. In a rather embarrassed
manner, he admitted that he had expected to be equally
as popular if not more popular than ever. He had not
succeeded. When he first came to the college campus, he
had been overcertain of himself and was accordingly not
liked by the other students. They did not invite him to the
fraternity parties and the college girls had treated him
somewhat coolly.

His attitude that the social affairs and outside activities
of a college are worthless was not his real attitude, even
though he may have firmly thought that it was. His arguments through which he had bolstered up his attitudes and
courage were psychological excuses, — rationalizations.

The person with queer ideas is one who has rationalized
a great deal. An excess of explaining, whether to ourselves
or others, is unhealthy mentally. Rationalizations deceive
ourselves even more than anyone else. People usually
rationalize when they do not have the courage to face
situations frankly and openly. They have to take refuge
behind some high sounding "reasons" which are simply
disguised excuses.

What are some of the excuses you have made today?

PERSONAL PROGRESS POINTERS

Am I too self-centered and forgetful of others in my de-
sire for progress?
Am I too emotional or too easy going?
Is my opinion of myself better than I merit?

CHAPTER XI

I

I DON'T know what will power is. But I do know that many people have difficulty in directing their mental and physical abilities consistently and effectively. Perhaps it is determination and grit they lack, perhaps it is a lack of will power. At any rate, they are lacking in a vital quality that makes for achievement. Near-poets are about the only people that can be a success with this lack in their make-up.

You may have known of people with such strong determination that they were privately called obstinate and stubborn. This is selfishness rather than the consistent direction of one's energies. It is not will power, but won't power. Many people think they are strong willed and moral merely because they do nothing bad. The real test, however, is not negative but positive. It is: how much good have you directed your energies to accomplish?

"May the gods spare me from these 'burn-'em-up' salesmen who work like a whirlwind the first week each month, and lay down the rest of the month," a sales manager of a Wall Street bond house said to me recently. He wanted bond salesmen who made most commissions for themselves—and incidentally for the company—at the end of the year, not those geniuses who could sell without trying and

[174]

who tried very sporadically. The race is not always won by the swiftest, but often by those with the rare quality of stick-to-itiveness.

The track coach of a midwestern university recently told me the following story which illustrates the point. Joe Smith came to college from the farm. He was too small to play football, too near-sighted to get into baseball or basket ball, but he wanted to serve the school and make a name for himself in track. But the track coach could see no signs of promise and Joe was advised to take up debating or checkers.

Discouraged, but still determined, Joe secretly trained himself for three years for the distances. Two miles from the campus where he lived was an attorney's home, and Joe took care of the furnace. Early mornings when no one was stirring about the campus he ran to his furnace. Late at night he repeated his morning program. He timed himself, varied his stride, and kept at it for three years without the coach being any the wiser.

When entries were being made for the spring meet of the conference Joe came out the first afternoon and showed the coach what he could do. The coach agreed to enter Joe in the two-mile distance. Joe held out, however, until he was entered for the half mile, mile, and two mile. He qualified in the preliminaries, and when the finals were run Joe came in first in each one.

I have fallen into the habit of thinking of Joe when I feel like running away to do something else. It helps me keep from becoming discouraged too easily. It helps me plan for results not just for a day but for a goal set several years into the future. I have found that it also helps others to know about Joe. Difficulties such as Joe surmounted really give the best experience there is for developing what some call will power.

II

There are several easily formed habits of work and thought which also give an added impetus to self-determination and energy direction. Get down to business at once is one of them. I know of people who actually tire themselves out in getting started to work. They listen for the clock to hear if it is running (although it has never missed a day). Then the things on top of their desk have to be arranged just so. Then they begin to wonder what they should do first. Suddenly they think it would be thoughtful to sharpen a supply of pencils. They should be made to realize, however, that it is better for them to grab the first letter and tend to that than indulge in all this will-weakening dalliance which each day gets a firmer hold through the tenacity of habit formation.

Another one of these important habits all should try to get deeply ingrained is to do the hard or unpleasant task the first thing. Continually postponing writing an unpleasant letter, for example, makes delaying it easier the next time. I have found personal desks literally crammed with unpleasant tasks of this nature. This particular person was not conscious of a weakening of his will; he was bothered with fatigue which his light job brought on. Little wonder! The accumulated worries in his desk would have tired anyone. Anticipating unpleasant tasks is thus not only undermining one's self-determination but is building up additional fatiguing worry as well. Do the difficult job first in the morning and enjoy a more restful day. Learn to like difficult tasks, for it is these rather than the easy ones that steel your determination.

III

How many unfinished jobs are left behind when we put on our hat to go home also indicates the strength of our self-determination. To develop this trait favorably one should stick to a job until it is done. Form the habit of staying, not quitting. And when you do feel like quitting think of Joe who trained for the distances, or Daguerre who spent fourteen years to get a photographic image to stick on glass. Don't be a putter-off.

The tired person is the weak-willed person who is easily led. Few people die from overwork, but many wills are killed in this fashion. The editor of one of the two best-known magazines in the world visited me last year. The first remark he made as he stepped off the train in Utica was, "For heaven's sake, don't ask me to make a decision; that is all I do all day long on the job and I want to rest." Form the habit of keeping well rested. If you need an alarm clock to get you started mornings, you are cheating yourself on rest.

Are you sold on yourself, on what you are doing, on the goal and aim you have in life? If you are, there is little need of worrying about your will being weak. The best incentives for getting determined and consistent action come from within. It is a sorry person who does not have his inner self goaded along by the example of some famous man of history or of today's business. Read about these people, associate with them as much as possible, and get under their shadow for personal encouragement and inspiration.

1. Form the habit of getting down to business at once.
2. Form the habit of doing the hard or unpleasant job first.
3. Form the habit of sticking to a job until it is done.

4. Keep well rested.

5. Believe in yourself, your job, your life plan.

PERSONAL PROGRESS POINTERS

What are some unpleasant tasks that I have been delaying? Why not clean them up at once?

Do I really try to like hard work?

Do I keep in proper physical condition so that I am not easily fatigued?

Do I have "too strong a will" and attempt to dominate others too much?

Why should I have confidence in myself?

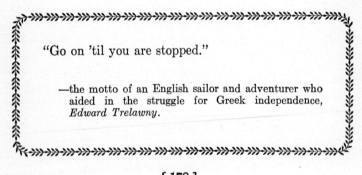

"Go on 'til you are stopped."

—the motto of an English sailor and adventurer who aided in the struggle for Greek independence, *Edward Trelawny*.

CHAPTER XII

I

ENGINEERS have improved this world remarkably in the last century; but I cannot find any authority to state that man himself has improved in the last two dozen centuries. In fact, if we believe the arguments of the eugenicists we might have to infer that mankind has actually deteriorated.

It is possible that we are on the threshold of an era which will accomplish for the human mind and personality what engineers have accomplished in our material world. Teachers are being thoroughly trained in modern psychology before they enter the classroom and come in contact with developing abilities and personalities—although it must be admitted that the old-fashioned school marm who simply loved children may have been much more successful in helping her pupils achieve their personality than are some of the products of our colleges who think they can accomplish the results by using a formula mechanically. But more later about trying to use a formula to solve personality problems. Great and growing numbers of foremen are receiving organized training in how to work with people; this agency, also, is going to accomplish a great deal toward helping the majority of people find personality achievement. Then there is the notable work of the National Committee for Mental Hygiene which as a center for education and propaganda has awakened widespread realization of

[179]

the importance of considering man's mentality and personality as impartially and as accurately as an engineer calculates the stresses and strains of a new skyscraper.

All these agencies will not, of course, improve the inborn nature of any of the present generation. And perhaps not of the next ten generations. But they can do tremendous things to help each of us come nearer to achieving the potentialities which are dormant within us. In the past generations there has been an appallingly wide gap separating what we might be capable of doing from what we actually had an opportunity to do. A gap fully as wide separated our happiness from the happiness we might have had. This gap represents a lack of self-realization. In numerous instances the lack of self-realization has been so great that almost a half million of our fellow citizens are under the care of the mental specialist. Undoubtedly there is another million who need such care, but do not realize it.

For us average people a program of mental hygiene focuses upon personality. With a successful personality adjustment even the pauper is a psychological success, and without a stable personality adjustment the millionaire is a psychological failure. But it is interesting to note in passing that the pauper and the millionaire are like Mr. Kipling's comments about Judy O'Grady and the Colonel's Lady. Psychologically, the personality twisting which makes one give up the struggle and seek refuge in the almshouse is very similar to the twisting which gives another man his powerful impulse to amass a great fortune, just to show that he can do it rather than making such an accumulation for the benefit of society. Neither has achieved his real personality potential. We may admire the one and pity the other, but our sympathies should be extended to both unless they have had the good fortune to achieve their best personality.

II

Brainy people seldom have good personalities. Feeble-minded people as a rule have unusual personality health. Personality is usually independent of one's intelligence and too much thinking can easily prevent the full blossom of emotional life which marks the well-integrated personality. The statement regarding brainy people needs a little quali-fying. People with slight personality unbalance often de-ceive many others into confusing unbalanced emotions with brains. This is especially noticeable in pseudo-literary and pseudo-artistic circles. But after allowing for these pa-thetically amusing cases, the fact remains that the aspira-tions and desires and abilities of the more intelligent are of such a character that they are more likely to be frus-trated and precipitate emotional irregularities.

This frustration is more likely to increase in the coming decades and bring individually disastrous results unless definite means are adopted for personality achievement. Walter B. Pitkin, of Columbia University, has just pub-lished a challenging study of the situation as he visions it for the year 1975. Half a century into the future he sees adequate employment for only half of the Best Minds. If he is right—and his figures are convincing—it will mean that many of our Best Minds will have to be content with occupation far below their abilities. This will demand a tremendous amount of personality adjustment.

The locus of personality adjustment is in the emotional life. Here are the most potent of our drives, and they appear to be both physical and mental. They may either paralyze or strengthen. They may lubricate the mental machinery, or they may throw sand in the bearings. They may make the stage-struck youth speechless on his first appearance, or they may yield to him unexpected powers of expression. Not all emotions are intense, some are mild and transitory as shown by our annoyance when some one is shelling peanuts behind us in the theater. Some are stable within the individual, varying little with season or occasion and giving a characteristic flavor to one's behavior that dominates in his personality. These give the basis for the personality traits of the individual that he must find an opportunity to express in his daily work and play—otherwise danger lurks in the abortive potential of dammed up emotional drives. At home, at work, or at school it is highly imperative that we find and be given avenues for living these trends—with the provision, of course, that previous damming has .not already given us emotional trends which are artificial. It is a matter not merely of being true to thine own self, but rather to thine own *best* self.

III

For a decade now I have been gathering data on some emotional groupings of very interesting nature. These are the groupings of the introvert, the ambivert, and the extravert. Dr. Carl J. Jung of Zurich first pointed out the peculiar grouping of emotional traits of the introvert and the extravert. Dr. Edmund S. Conklin discovered the great middle group now known as ambiverts, who are neither introvert nor extravert but a little of each. This is a highly practical classification, although it obviously does not tell *all* that is worth knowing about one's personality. It describes, however, probably one of the most important sectors of personality.

The extravert has been called the man of action; the introvert, the man of thought. Extraverts have been called practical minded; introverts have been called dreamers.

The extraverts express their emotions by living them; the introverts repress their emotions into the sphere of their own consciousness. Poets and philosophers are introverted. Go-getters and affable salesmen are extraverts. Youth is relatively extraverted; age is relatively introverted. In the animal kingdom Airedales may be looked upon as extraverts and Persian cats as introverts—although this may not mean much to the cat!

The great in-between group with about an equal mixture of the traits of both the introvert and extravert are the ambiverts. Fully half of us are ambiverts. And in consequence fully half of us are likely to have unusual trouble in achieving personality expression in the future years, as we will see shortly.

A list of 48 traits that reveal different degrees of introversion-extraversion have been experimented upon in the Colgate psychological laboratory during the past five years. As the fruit of this painstaking research by a great number of students in this laboratory, we have evolved a simple mental test for introversion-extraversion which is now in use on a large scale in more than two hundred schools, clinics, and industries. More than 100,000 people have been tested with the aid of these forms. I hope most of these have had their personality achievement furthered in the light of their test results.

Before outlining a brief and simplified form of this test it should be definitely understood that introverts are just as desirable as extraverts. Both are definitely needed in the present scheme of things. Both have their weak points. The vital question is not, which type is most praiseworthy and which should I try to be? The vital question is, which do I approximate closest, and how can I achieve the best expression of this make-up? The president of General Motors is of one extreme, the president of General Electric is of the other, yet neither is out of place in our world. Will Rogers is one extreme, Charles A. Lindbergh is the other. So with Alfred Smith and Herbert Hoover.

Those who show up as introvert on this check list can take pride in numbering yourselves in the following distinguished group: Nathaniel Hawthorne, Joan of Arc, Edgar Allan Poe, Michelangelo, and Eleanore Duse. Those who show up as extravert can seek consolation in sharing this distinction with Douglas Fairbanks, the Prince of Wales, Queen Marie, Phyllis Haver, Theodore Roosevelt, Sr., and Helen Wills. To the great in-betweens—the ambiverts—we will allow the emotional companionship of Sherwood Anderson, Charlie Chaplin, the last Czar of Russia, Pola Negri, Greta Garbo, and Sarah Bernhardt. Neither type is without distinguished and charming company, although in anticipation it might be stated that one usually finds his own type the most pleasing company.

IV

Now, that there will be no hard feelings let us see what the outstanding traits are that indicate these personality aggregates. These questions have been framed so that an answer of "yes" indicates introversion, an answer of "no" indicating extraversion. If yesses predominate in your answers, introversion predominates in your make-up; if noes predominate, extraversion predominates in your make-up. If the difference between your yesses and your noes is not marked you join the group with Charlie Chaplin and Greta Garbo!

1. Are you inclined to think about misfortunes, or to anticipate misfortunes? The introvert worries because it is the most natural thing in the world for him to do, and the extravert does not worry for the same reason. So we should

greatly discount the alarums of the introverts and the lack of alarum of the extravert.

2. Are your feelings easily hurt by remarks or actions referring to you, or which you think refer to you? The moral of this is never to give an introvert the slightest cause for offense, and if you happen to be an extravert you have probably been overlooking many intended affronts. Obviously it is an exceptional introvert that can withstand the affronts of politics.

3. Are you inclined to be outspoken and to express your opinions? Do you perhaps take pride in calling a spade a spade, regardless of how the other fellow may feel about it? It is a strange contrast that the extravert who has relatively numb feelings is at the same time the one who is most careful of the feelings of others. As a practical application of this I know one executive who greatly discounts letters of recommendation written by those he judges to be extravert.

4. Do you usually like to find some good reason for deciding to do something? The introvert aims to be meticulously logical. The extravert just decides and does not bother to explain why, either to himself or to others. It is a time-consuming activity on the part of the introvert, and often a logical loss on the part of the extravert. This is one reason why the introvert is likely to be dressed in better taste but in longer time than the extravert.

5. Are you inclined to rebel when given orders or told to do something? It is probably the more introverted doughboys who wanted to hang their second lieutenant. Care must be used in dealing with introvert school children or adults not to give them orders directly. There is no use trying to convince them why they should take orders—it is just not their nature. So give orders indirectly.

6. Do you have a tendency to work better, or to think it

[185]

over seriously when you are praised? Praise is wasted on the extravert—salesmen want bonuses or commissions or prizes, not praise. But the introvert would rather have a few praising words than a raise in pay. This introvert trait is more common among women, and I trust husbands will see the immediate applications.

7. Are you somewhat bookish? Do you prefer the editorial page to the sports page? In general, introverts have bookish or intellectual interests, while the extraverts are permeated with athletic interests. Since college professors are usually introvert and students not so introvert, is it little wonder that they are perennially at odds over the relative importance of athletics?

8. Are you a good loser? The extravert is, but the introvert takes his losses seriously. The extravert does not pause to explain why he overbid his bridge hand—but blithely goes ahead and overbids his next hand. The extravert is the poker sharper's cause for rejoicing—the introvert is likely to call in the police in retaliation. Also, never outargue an introvert—he is a poor loser, and also it is usually impossible to outargue him!

9. Do you prefer to work alone? Groups and even mobs are the extravert's delight; solitude, even loneliness, the delight of the introvert. Small towns are the Mecca of the introvert, and even Times Square is too sparsely populated for the classical extravert. Turn the introvert's desk so he faces the wall rather than a room crowded with workers, and he will work much happier. One-man concerns are for the introvert, while the extravert is content to merge thousands.

10. Do you prefer delicate, painstaking work? Die and tool makers, watchmakers, laboratory technicians find their most enthusiastic workers among the introverts. The extravert is likely to throw up such a job at the first chance,

[186]

and really not know why he did not like it. Look for spelling difficulties among the extraverts—it is just too much trouble for them to give attention to detail.

11. Are you inclined to choose associates of less accomplishment and ability than you? Perhaps the introvert is cleverly protecting himself from criticism by picking associates he can easily lead and dominate. And we are undoubtedly unfair in calling the extravert a "climber" when it is just his emotional make-up to choose as associates those superior to him.

12. Do you express yourself better in writing than in speaking? Washington Irving was tongue-tied as an orator—introverted also. Patrick Henry was incoherent as a letter writer, but he could sway the early congresses in a typically extravert fashion. Yet public speaking is required of many college students—rubbing in the already present weakness of the introvert, just as English composition goes against the grain of the extravert. Psychologically there is little justification in these attempts to reduce all to the same pattern.

13. Do you like to keep in the background at social affairs? It is easy for the introvert to discover some reason why he should not accept invitations, and the extravert is likely to be organizing a party with no other reason than he would like one.

14. Do you hesitate to loan money or other possessions? The introvert is both a poor borrower and a poor lender. The extravert is at the other extreme in both, except as a borrower he is likely to forget to return the borrowed articles for an indefinite period. This is one trait in which women are more extravert than men, and it is a safe generalization to try to borrow first from your sister rather than from your brother. An example of this is to be noted in the way women exchange dresses.

15. Are you especially careful about your property, the polish of your car, the arrangement of your dresser drawer, the repair of your clothing? The automobile that has never been washed and that has always been in need of oiling is probably driven by an extravert. Habits of tidiness do not have to be encouraged among the introverts, they already have them. And to encourage such habits among extraverts is rather working against nature.

16. Do you have only slight interest in the opposite sex? Bachelors and old-maids-by-choice are recruited from the introverts. And the heart affairs of traveling salesmen have for years been a subject of both song and story. Contrary to popular opinion, we have found that most capable actors and actresses, such as Robert Mantell, are introverted, while only the chorus people are extraverted.

17. Are you fond of discussion or argument? Paraphrasing the statement that when Greek meets Greek they start a restaurant, we may say that when introvert meets introvert they start an argument; and both are sublimely happy. The extravert merely changes the subject, he is not partial to argumentation.

18. Are you careful about making friends? The coldness of small New England villages is due more to the introversion of the inhabitants than to any ill-experience with strangers. Extraverts are more successful politically because they are naturally friendly with almost everyone.

19. And do you blush easily? The extravert probably did not blush at the mention of the traveling salesmen a few moments ago.

There is a somewhat detailed picture of the introvert and the extravert. We could find plenty of flaws with each so-called type but for the pragmatic fact that all combinations seem to fulfill an important place in this world. For instance, a few years ago I recommended a student for work with a corporation solely on the basis of his great penchant for criticism and argumentation. "This office is becoming too self-satisfied," the manager had written me previously. This young college man changed that quickly!

v

I am often asked if one can change from an introvert to an extravert. The answer is "Yes, much easier than from an extravert into an introvert. But why change? It is not worth the effort or the hazard!" More important than changing one's personality spots is to find vocational and recreational outlets for these. Achieve outlets for these personality trends, do not try to thwart them unless on expert advice you are told that they are undesirable. At the present moment some of them may appear undesirable to you, but that is likely to be because you are in work or among friends that make you try to dam their expression. Be true to thine own best self, but do not take false pride in trying to be different.

At the professional level, the indications are that there is ample opportunity for the introvert, ambivert, or extravert to be his natural self and at the same time to be successful as measured by worldly standards. Since all professions presume intensive educational preparation, the introvert is placed at advantage in being more of what is known as a student type. On the other hand, success in these lines involves sales strategy in its most subtle forms, and often the extravert has the advantage after the diplomas are awarded. Some of the best professional skill is buried under apparent mediocrity due to a lack of this natural and unintentional salesmanship.

The housewife in isolated daily routine is more satisfying to the introvert, yet both have to be housewives in the present scheme of things, although woman is entering industry in increasing numbers.

VI

When we turn to the industrial and business world we find a challenging situation. Except in one-man businesses it is usually either the introvert or the extravert who has the most natural opportunity for achieving his personality, the one for the details of manufacture and development, the other for the exploitation of the products the introvert has developed. Danger lurks in this trend in our civilization. I am not thinking of the danger of a resentful radicalism on the part of the sensitive introvert development engineer over the large earnings of a sales manager he saw flunk out of college. The real danger lurks in the ambivert being on the verge of finding himself without a chance to be his natural self or to find an adequate outlet for his dominant personality traits in his daily work.

And most of us are ambiverts!

Are these forces going to continue so that the ambivert will find his personality drives dammed so that they seek hazardous indirect outlets? Or will natural forces such as labor turnover prevent further encroachment into this great ambivert group. If they do not we can easily see great numbers of personalities thwarted.

"Know thyself," said Socrates, and that was excellent psychological advice—but it did not go far enough.

"Be yourself," was the advice of Marcus Aurelius, and thus the Latin improved on the Greek.

But it remained for St. Paul to strike the correct and complete psychological note when he wrote to Timothy, "Neglect not the gift which is in thee."

And neglect not the gift which is in others!

PERSONAL PROGRESS POINTERS

What are my outstanding personality traits? Does this analysis fit my daily work? Have I outlets in recreation for those that are not called into play in my work?

Which of my personality traits are the ones that appear to be a handicap and which I will attempt to improve?

Am I able to appreciate the personality traits of others, regardless of how different they may be from mine?

What personality traits should I strengthen to prepare for a promotion?

What are the most favorable personality traits of some people I dislike?

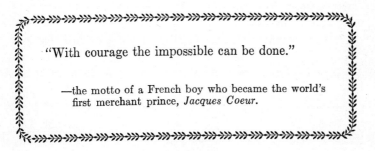

"With courage the impossible can be done."

—the motto of a French boy who became the world's first merchant prince, *Jacques Coeur*.

CHAPTER XIII

TWO DOZEN WAYS TO KEEP SANE

I

A few days ago a student came to me, glanced around the laboratory, and asked if anyone could hear us.

"Doc, I'm worried. A cousin of mine, school teacher at Evanston, has been acting funny for some time. Saw her last summer and was struck by her queerness."

"Now," he continued with effort, "they've had to take her to a private sanitarium and they don't know if she will recover. For a while she is very happy and excited, then she gradually becomes glum and gloomy and will sit around weeping for a week."

It appeared to be a case of what is known as manic-depressive mental disorder.

"About one-fourth of people who have mental disorder recover," I said, trying to encourage him.

"But think of the family, even if she is one of the fortunate fourth," he countered.

"You mean ——"

"If this thing is in the family any of us might have a breakdown like that!"

He voiced a common opinion, one that causes much mental anguish, and one for which there is but scant, if any, foundation.

From the bookshelf just back of my chair I took Dr. Abraham Myerson's new book on the inheritance of mental diseases. I told the student how Dr. Myerson had found little basis for the belief that mental disorder was inherited. It may run in families, but for reasons other than "bad blood."

"Your cousin who is mentally ill may have a bad effect on the family," I said, "if the family worries about heredity. It is the worry, not the heredity that is bad!

"Feeblemindedness does run in families. But your cousin was not feebleminded, for she was a school teacher. You are not feebleminded because you read magazines and newspapers readily.

"There is nothing especially unusual about your cousin," I continued. "Last year there were almost as many persons admitted to mental hospitals as there are in the Silver State of Nevada; more than there are in the great steel city of Gary.

"It is not heredity, but ways of thinking and ways of living, that caused most of these mental breakdowns. Your cousin probably was not bothered by her way of living."

He nodded assent.

"In her ways of thinking?"

"She always was prudish, but that was her parents' fault. They would not let her go with fellows when she was in college and had her upset most of the time about the sins of the world," he said. "They let her have no close friends. If she was not home from her teaching by four o'clock her mother went after her. Her mother went with her whenever she had to be out evenings."

"Now does that sound like bad heredity or a foolish mother?" I asked.

"I think I'd go off the handle myself if I had to live like that," was his reply.

And I agreed with him inwardly!

There are many living under similar intolerable situations.

II

This girl of twenty-eight had not suddenly "lost her mind." For years she had been slipping. People do not suddenly loose their mental control. It is a gradual process and in many cases it appears possible to check the development before it has gone too far.

One is not born that way; one gets that way. There are two dozen good rules to prevent getting that way which I use in my mental hygiene work with students, a surprising number of whom seem to be well along toward getting that way.

These rules are:

1. Avoid alcohol to any excess. About 5 per cent of mental disorder is due directly to alcoholic excesses. Women are not afflicted with alcoholic psychoses—as breakdowns due to this cause are called—as frequently as are men. But they do occur with regrettable commonness among women who appear to be as susceptible to the disastrous influences as are men.

2. Avoid social disease. One out of every ten mental patients is taken to wards with paresis, which is caused solely by social disease. Five years ago this form of mental disorder was considered incurable and after a few years with the disorder death invariably followed. Advances in treatment during the last few years, however, are bringing about wonderful cures.

Not all mental disorders can be so remarkably relieved, however. The ounce of prevention by right thinking and right living still beats a ton of cure in most cases.

3. Keep physically fit. At the Trenton, New Jersey, State Hospital Dr. Cotton is bringing about what appear to be phenomenal recoveries by removing points of infection in the body. A good rule is to have a complete medi-

[194]

cal examination on every birthday, including X-ray examination for hidden infections. Exercise of a vigorous kind out in the open should be taken every day. If you were to visit a mental hospital, you would find the patients taken outdoors for a walk two hours each forenoon and again two hours each afternoon. At the Chicago State Hospital you would find a gymnasium instructor prescribing exercises for patients.

4. Avoid hunting for reasons to justify everything you do. Most of the activities of daily life are so unimportant that it does not matter whether you wear this necktie or that one. Still there are many people who spend a long time deciding which tie to wear, which thing to do first, whether to start a letter "Dear Sirs" or "Gentlemen."

Accept your decisions without quibbling, and do not bore others or handicap yourself by continually explaining just *why* you did just *what* you did.

5. Mingle freely with others. Do not be socially backward. Do not be a recluse who lives in a world of fancy rather than in the world of reality. Avoid even a tendency in this direction. Take in some social gathering at least once a week. Drop in some evening and visit neighbors. Be a social being and you'll be a healthier person mentally.

6. Do not be afraid to express your emotions. Let your feelings of joy, admiration, dislike, and enthusiasm be known. If you do not feel these, you'll be surprised to find how soon they can be acquired if you merely pretend a little admiration and enthusiasm. Is there some national figure for whom you show admiration? Some civic activity in your community about which you are enthusiastic? By all means find some if you do not have them now!

7. Keep your stronger emotions under control. Anger, hatred, and sex cannot be entirely crowded out of one's mental life, but they should be guided as a spirited horse. You do not try to keep the horse motionless, but rather to

guide him with a tight rein. So with these more spirited emotions. Accept these emotions as natural, but always try to control and direct them.

8. Recognize that work under pressure and hurry is not necessary in modern life. Have you really tried to be easy-going for an hour or two each day?

9. Learn how to relax and rest, both mentally and physically. The farmer's horse relaxes during the work whenever his master releases the reins. Many moderns do not have this horse sense.

10. Do not work by fits and starts. Do not alternate extreme work with rest. Work steadily and consistently, and work becomes easier.

11. Play as well as work. But keep the two separate. Do you know how to enjoy a concert, outdoor exercise, reading, the theater? Each day you should have several hours' diversion of one of these sorts, diversion different from the work of the day.

12. Realize that you are not an exception. Others have the same trials, the same human weaknesses, the same failures. You are not the most unlucky person, your problems are not different from anyone else's. This does not imply to give up, but rather to recognize that after all there is nothing unusual about it, or about yourself, for that matter.

13. Have some close friends. Marriage seems to be the only way some can gain a close friend, and from this does marriage win the special support of the mental hygienist. Friendship, however, requires both give and take, it demands personal sacrifices at times.

14. Talk over your troubles. You have many little irritations which do not merit the dignity of "trouble." But when troubles arise take them to your friend, your family, or your priest and talk them over. Don't try to forget them, don't shirk them, don't spend useless worry over them: talk them over with some one.

15. Avoid keeping things to yourself. The secretive person gets nowhere, and his secretiveness may help get him into the mental hospital.

16. The gossip who tells all he knows—and some that he does not know—is as harmful to himself as his opposite, the secretive person. There is a balance which we can all achieve.

17. Do nothing which you may later regret and worry over. The easiest way to choke off worry is at its source.

18. Don't be a prude. And at the same time do not be a rake. Acknowledge the biological necessity and imperativeness of sex.

19. Don't have a New England conscience. Do not make a moral mountain out of the molehills of everyday conduct. Be moral, think morally, but don't make a moral issue out of everything. Be habitually moral so you do not have to have the New England conscience.

20. Be considerate of the feelings of others. Outspokenness, a tendency to belittle others, to slur them, is a close relative of the mental patient.

21. Do not be suspicious of the motives and morals of others. The school teacher with whom we started this article failed in this, but she had been raised that way by her parents. Others are not trying to get the best of you and are not moral degenerates. Be a Quaker and always give the benefit of the doubt.

22. Set a reasonable goal for your ambition—one that it is possible to attain. Forget the mansion and servants, set your goal on a six-room bungalow, a cheap car, a steady job, the respect of others. You can find happiness and success where you are and in simple things.

23. Have some hobbies. Flowers, poultry, fishing, saving, helping. Have hobbies in which you *do* something, not merely *think* about them.

24. Forget your heredity. One person is responsible for you—you.

PERSONAL PROGRESS POINTERS

Am I needlessly worrying about my heredity—or, perhaps, taking too much pride in it?

Do I have some close friends to whom I can unburden my troubles sympathetically?

Do I have a hobby or two which require action rather than largely thought? What hobby could I take up to good advantage?

Have I planned my ambitions at a sensible, reasonable, possible mark?

What sort of a mental environment am I setting up for myself and the members of my family?

Am I keeping physically and morally fit, without becoming a faddist or a prude?

"Yesterday is but a Dream,
Tomorrow is only a Vision,
But today well lived makes
Every yesterday a Dream of Happiness,
And every tomorrow a Vision of Hope."

—Favorite verse, from the Sanskrit, of a Canadian backwoods boy who became the world's leading physician, *Sir William Osler*.

CHAPTER XIV

THE BATTLE WITH FATIGUE

I

THE longer one is on the job the more fatigued he feels although experiments upon those writing checks in a railroad auditor's office have shown that the clerks write about as many checks the last hour as they did the first. How tired one feels is really no indication of how much work he can do. Usually, one slacks up when he is beginning to feel tired, but he can still do as much work as he formerly did, if he only knew it.

Other sorts of work show the same inconsistency between the way one *feels* he can work and the way he really *can* work.

Work that is almost purely mental, such as multiplying four place numbers like 5,376 and 9,727 in the head without using paper or pencil, shows the same deceptive feeling of fatigue. Physical work such as carrying bricks or folding handkerchiefs for eight hours or more steadily has produced similar results.

You cannot tell by looking at a horse how fast he can run or how big a load he can haul. Nor can you tell by how tired you seem to feel whether you are fatigued or not. Usually one is not as fatigued as he imagines.

II

Fatigue may be caused by bodily conditions of which we are not aware, but which still take a severe toll from one.

If you have tired spells, if you cannot keep up the pace with others, if you have aches and pains, if the last hour or two of the day finds you sluggish and fatigued — have a medical examination. You may never have been ill a day in your life but your strength may be below par.

A letter addressed to the Life Extension Institute, 25 West Forty-third Street, New York City, will bring you information about the excellent health service they maintain for well people. They will tell you of a physician near your home who is qualified to make a *health* examination and give you necessary advice.

My battle against fatigue has underlying it a thorough examination by one of the Life Extension Institute's physicians each year. I know after that that most of my sense of fatigue is not organic but somewhat imaginary, although I do not like to call it imaginary because it is more disastrous at times than that originating in bodily disturbances.

III

The purpose of *real* fatigue seems to be to protect us from overexertion. It is not caused by exhaustion, but prevents exhaustion. It is sort of a safety valve provided by Nature, but one which most of us have set to blow-off under a pressure so low that our daily efficiency is actually impeded.

Did you ever awake in the morning feeling more tired than you did when you went to bed? Are these feelings of fatigue a result of overwork? Do they serve to protect your body from exhaustion? Not a bit of it. They have a protective value, but they do not come from work or even from physical causes. It is to such ultra-deceptive fatigue as this that we shall now turn our attention.

When we take up this "tired feeling" without work or exertion to cause it, we shall first have to pass in hasty review some diseases about which much has been learned

[200]

within recent years. This "tired feeling" is not due to kidney disorders as the patent medicine advertisements would have us believe. These advertisements are capitalizing symptoms that many people have. The medicine may help but more likely it may not. Thousands of bottles can be sold, however, since their appeal is to humanity's most common ailment — that "tired feeling."

IV

The disease that will give us the most insight into this "tired feeling" is known as *hysteria*. The disease, hysteria, is not exactly what most folks think of when they hear the word. In everyday parlance, we think of the hysterical person as the one who indulges in loud, senseless laughter at the wrong time, has a bad temper, or is nervous and afraid of the dark. These actions are not of the sort of which the scientist thinks when he hears the word.

The symptoms of hysteria are numerous, and every one of them is of immense importance in modifying everyday efficiency. Blindness is sometimes caused by hysteria. A person may become unable to use his limbs, or he may become subject to fits, or his body may be strangely twisted out of shape. These are some of the symptoms of hysteria.

The significant fact about this disease is that, in spite of the apparent severity of the symptoms, not one of them is a real disorder. Every symptom might be called "faked," that is, there is really no organic disturbance. By some queer twist in human affairs, these symptoms gradually develop without there being any genuine organic cause for them.

The rest cure for "nervous exhaustion" was based upon a misconception of these tired feelings. The nerve cells are not exhausted; they are as well nourished as ever.

The trouble lies in the mind that causes them to work in strange and unseeming ways.

But the symptoms are there. There is no denying this fact. And, moreover, the patients with hysteria are not intentionally faking their blindness or their paralysis. So far as the patients are concerned, their ailments are real.

Neither is there any denying the fact that there is no real basis for the symptoms, so far as the patient's condition is concerned. This is what has made hysteria an enigma for centuries. All sorts of theories have been seriously advanced in an attempt to understand this peculiar disease. It is only recently that scientists have discovered that there is actually no basis for the disease in the patient's body, and that the cause back of the symptoms is mental. When we have this cause disclosed, we can understand the source of many of these feelings of fatigue which have no bodily basis.

There is no doubt but that the symptoms of the hysterical patient are not real. An hysterical paralytic who has not walked for years still suffers no withering of the muscles of the legs as would have occurred if it had been a genuine paralysis. The reflex movements of the leg are disordered in certain forms of real paralysis. When the bottom of the foot is lightly tickled, for example, all the toes except the great toe flex downward but the great toe goes in the opposite direction. This is the normal reflex. In hysterics, it is unmodified. But in certain cases of real paralysis, the great toe falls in line with the others and bends downward as they do. This is another simple test by which experts can determine whether a disease is real or not. Paralyzed muscles react differently to electricity than do normal ones, but the apparently paralyzed muscles of the hysteric react the same as do normal muscles.

There is no fooling the specialist about the nature of a disease. But the average person may be convinced sooner with signs less technical than these, which indicate that hysterical affections are not real bodily affections.

Hysterical blindness is a good example. Patients who grope their way about and who cannot see their food suddenly receive their sight back again when the hospital catches fire or when some exciting incident occurs. Similarly, hysterics who were apparently deaf have been made to hear by suddenly whispering to them while on a walk through the gardens, "Look out for that snake!"

At a recent fire in a government veteran's hospital, an ex-soldier who was a victim of hysteria and apparently completely paralzed suddenly recovered and shocked the other patients when he climbed to the roof of the building during the fire!

So much for the symptoms and the deceptive nature of hysteria. It has been found to be much like our feelings of apparent fatigue. Let us see now what brings about the peculiar condition of the hysterical patient. An actual case will be the most interesting.

A woman came into a physician's office complaining of a pain in her arm. Ordinarily, the physician would have asked her if she had been out in damp weather, or if she had been troubled with rheumatism, and according to her answers would have prescribed some salycilates. But this physician had been trained in just such deceptive symptoms as we have been discussing. He made a careful study of the case and found that it was not her arm that was troubling her but an experience out of the past.

This woman was approaching middle life, and she was unmarried. Several years previously, she had started keeping company with a young man. They were mutually devoted to each other. But he did not propose although their friends believed them engaged and she inwardly thought that some day they would be. After graduation, he obtained a position in a distant city but kept in constant touch with her. Each vacation he spent much of his time with her.

Why he did not propose marriage she could not understand. One day she received a letter from him saying that he had received a substantial raise in salary. Then, she thought that he would surely marry her. All her friends, when they heard about the promotion, were also certain that now the marriage was merely a matter of a short time.

When his vacation came following the raise, he spent most of the time with her as usual. Each day she expected the long anticipated proposal of marriage, but for some reason it was not forthcoming.

After he had left to return to his work, the whole family was disgusted. The girl was terribly disappointed. Soon afterwards, she began feeling the pain in her arm. She was not striving for sympathy in this ailment without any physical basis. She was suffering from the past. The pain in her arm was a remembrance of the last evening the engineer had spent with her and the slight pressure he had exerted on her arm as they were walking together through the garden. At that time, she had expected the long awaited proposal, only to suffer keen disappointment.

This symptom was thus found to be due to a lingering hope. It was, in a certain sense, a flight from reality. The young man had manifested no desire for marriage, but the pressure on the arm could be interpreted as signifying affection. So her hopes had lingered and they had been encouraged by developing this pain in her arm.

It must not be interpreted that this patient *intentionally* feigned this disorder. It was as real to her as real could be. She was just a victim of a trick played on her by her own mental life, working at levels of which she was not aware.

These mental tricks are also the same ones that are at

work adding to our fatigue, or in producing fatigue after only a little exertion.

V

How can a cure be affected? Very simply but, at the same time, in a most surprising way. When the patient has explained to the physician what the cause of this peculiar condition is, the disorder suddenly disappears almost as it came — out of a clear sky. The patient, for instance, who had a pain in her arm suffered no more after the mental experience back of the symptom had been discovered.

Dr. Brill tells of a woman who was unable to walk. After sufficient study, he found that her's was an hysterical paralysis, and also unearthed the precise reason why this symptom had developed. He explained it all to her and she laughingly stated that she would never be made to walk by such a simple means! But she walked home!

What has all this about peculiar folks with peculiar diseases to do with "that tired feeling" you have at times?

Another case of Dr. Brill's will be helpful. This concerns a woman who began to write a letter one morning. Previously, she had been perfectly well. She had scarcely written the date when she was seized with a feeling of sadness, and was unable to proceed with the letter or efficiently with any other work. Analysis of her case revealed the fact that the date touched off, as it were, certain unpleasant experiences of her past which had happened on the same date.

We are not picking on the women. Just as many examples could be given of hysterical affections among men. As a matter of fact, this is precisely what "shell shock" is. It is not an organic or bodily disease brought about by the high explosives but a sort of flight from reality, a protection from the unpleasant, by mentally inducing apparent paralysis, tremors, blindnesses, and all the complex and assorted symptoms of hysteria.

What is called "railroad paralysis" is another kind of hysterical affection. Soon after a favorable verdict is rendered, the control of the limbs is oftentimes *miraculously* recovered. The chief surgeon of a prominent western railroad tells the story of a person who had been injured in a wreck and paralyzed from the hips down. A long suit at law followed which ended with a verdict against the company. The plaintiff was so elated that he *walked* to the jury box and thanked the foreman for his verdict!

That "tired feeling" is a close relative of hysteria and is known as *neurasthenia*, when it is apparent bodily fatigue, or as *psychasthenia*, when it is apparent mental fatigue. In neither of these is there actual fatigue or any real bodily disturbance. The nerves are sound and the muscles are healthy but, within the head, some past experience, hope, or ambition is cherished and disguised in the form of fatigue.

The best cure for these spurious fatigues is a mental prophylaxis—a frank facing of the thwartings of each day, freedom in confiding troubles and aspirations to a close friend, and in general a close adherence to the rules given elsewhere in this book on how to keep emotional health. Regulate your life so that excessive fatigue is avoided and take tiredness after ten waking hours as perfectly natural.

VI

Did you ever notice how prevalent "housewife's headache" is on washing and ironing days — not from actual overwork or overheat but from causes which will be laid bare in a moment? And did you ever notice how the laborer comes home more fatigued than ever when he has been called down or when someone else has received a raise? And did you ever notice how the business man is too tired to play golf after a "hard day's work" when cotton has dropped a dozen points?

Saying that these common feelings of fatigue are mental does not mean that they are entirely imaginary. They can be removed and avoided by knowing their real cause which for each person is an individual matter. He has to determine it for himself or else consult a qualified specialist. Merely to deny the existence of the "tired feeling" is grossly inadequate. The whole thing must be uprooted bodily and exposed to conscious inspection. Only then is the source eliminated and further trouble avoided.

In each case it is an individual matter, but a few type cases will be of value. Such, for instance, is the woman who gradually finds herself bored and fatigued by doing a little light housework. She had been disillusioned by a hasty marriage, but the "tired feeling" did not develop until the wife of a former sweetheart of her's had succumbed to influenza.

Another instance is that of a young college graduate who had literary aspirations. He joined the staff of a newspaper after graduation and, during his evenings, he worked on short stories which he sent to the editors of some of the leading magazines. Soon his proffered contributions began to come back. He lost interest in his newspaper work and became more and more neurasthenic. He was tired, unable to think for any length of time, and became indolent, living off his aged and none too comfortably fixed parents.

Another case is that of a striking shopman who had been employed on a railroad that did not settle with the unions. Although he had not worked for several months, he gradually developed that "tired feeling" which became worse and worse until he was given sick benefits. As soon as the strike on his road had been settled and he saw a possibility of getting out of debt, he returned to his work and the feeling of fatigue disappeared.

An opera singer, who had been the star of a small municipal organization for several years, saw her position of prestige waning with the coming of a new recruit to the company. She gradually developed that "tired feeling" until it was no longer possible for her to appear on the program. When the new songster was dismissed for indiscretions of conduct, the old star recovered from her neurasthenia and returned to an active operatic life.

These illustrations could be multiplied. On very hand, we find examples of the falseness of that "tired feeling." Real fatigue may be nature's device to protect our bodies from overwork, but the common fatigue of everyday life is largely a deceiver.

That "tired feeling" results from taking something too seriously. It can be eliminated mainly by finding out what that something is.

Next to understanding what the cause of that "tired feeling" is, a stiff job is a good remedy to employ. Occupation plus enthusiasm causes the dissolution of fatigue. The most fatigued folks are those who do nothing but sit and fret about their hard lot and the strenuousness of life. France's Fighting Woman Doctor was not of this calibre. As Dorothy Canfield wrote about Dr. Girard-Mangin, she was a little woman, "not very strong, slightly built, with some serious constitutional weaknesses." Yet under the patriotic enthusiasms of war read this about her:

"Think of her out there in her leaky, makeshift hospital, with her twenty crude helpers, and her hundreds of mortally sick typhoid patients; four hundred and seventy days of continuous service with no place to sleep — when there was a chance — except in a freezing, wind-swept attic in a deserted village. Think of her in the midst of that terrible battle of Verdun, during four black nights without a light, among those delirious men, and then during the long, long ride with her dying patients over the shell-swept roads. Listen to her as she speaks of herself at the end of that ride, without a place to lay her head: 'Oh, how tired I was, as I went dragging myself from door to door begging for a room and bed. It was because I was no longer working, you see. As long as you have work to do you can go on.'

"Then listen to her as she receives her orders to rush to a new post, before she has had time to lay herself on the bed she finally found. 'Then at once my tiredness went away. It only lasted while I thought of getting to bed. When I knew we were going into action once more, I was myself again.'

"Watch her as she rides on through the afternoon and the long, dangerous night; as she swallows her coffee and plum-cake, and operates for five hours without stopping; as she sleeps in the only place there is — a quite comfortable chair in a corner; and as she keeps up this life for twenty days before she is sent — not on a vacation, mind you, but to another strenuous post."

As long as you have work to do you can go on!

PERSONAL PROGRESS POINTERS

Have I had a physician examine me to see if some bodily condition is hampering my progress?

Do I tell others how tired I am?

Do I enjoy telling them?

How can I acquire more enthusiasm for my work?

CHAPTER XV

LESS FATIGUE FROM BETTER POSTURE

I

A MANUFACTURER wanted me to size up chairs for him to help select ones which would eliminate all possible fatigue. I have just finished working through more than 150 hard-to-read scientific reports on posture in an effort to give him the help he wanted—and also partly so I could sit better and stand better myself. With his permission I am letting you see my report to him, so here it is:

I was astonished to find that in order to sit or stand scientifically I had to know something about bears, penguins, babies' spines, and how 65 per cent of the geniuses of the world have worked. I also made the great discovery that man is the only animal which spits, and that this is due to his posture!

There is no other animal which persistently walks in the vertical position. Bears walk in this upright position from time to time, and once in a while some birds, such as the penguin, strut around in this position, but man is the only one who sticks to it through thick and thin.

I would advise my neighbor against training his dog to sit up or walk on his hind legs after all this reading. If using this vertical body position is as hard on the dog as specialists say it has been on man, my neighbor would actually be cruel to his pet.

Man, from this point of view, is an animal built inwardly

for living with his trunk in a horizontal position parallel with the surface of the earth but in whom perverse habit makes him go against the way Nature intended him to and walks upright, with his trunk vertical to the surface of the earth.

Dr. Ales Hrdlica, the distinguished anthropologist of the Smithsonian Institution, has aroused a great deal of interest the last few months in his collection of modern instances of boys and girls who have walked around on all fours like little kittens until they were so old that their parents were actually worried in many cases. These children offer additional evidence that man was designed as an engineering product to go around horizontally, but he deigned to become upright.

There are valves in our veins, for instance, which function best when we are in the horizontal posture. If we walked on all fours, the appendix would not clog up and precipitate a hospital bill. The colon has to work against gravity in the upright trunk. There is more danger of brain hemorrhage in the vertical position of the trunk, as well as increased susceptibility to varicose veins.

Man has been changed in appearance by his upright position. It has given his spine two curves so that it resembles an elongated letter "S" while other animals have a spine with a single curve resembling a stretched-out "C." The reverse curve we have acquired in our spines makes it easier to balance the trunk on the big femur bones of the leg by moving the center of gravity of the trunk back a few inches. The year-old child has only the single curve in its spine, but as soon as it begins to walk the additional curve makes its appearance.

Big feet, stronger heels, arches developed, and a larger great toe are the price we have to pay at one end for this erect posture.

At the other end of the body there have been one or two

outstanding advantages resulting from man's typical posture. The range of vision and hearing was enormously increased, while the lower animals still depend almost entirely upon smell and taste. The drainage from the brain is vastly better due to the upright position of the body.

The bony sinuses are drained better, however, in the horizontal position, and as a result of walking and sitting man has brought on conditions which encourage sinus infections, the most painful infection that can be experienced. Diseases of the ear and mastoid are also aggravated in man.

Within the trunk itself we discover that the upright posture encourages all the mysterious and important insides to sag an inch or more, encouraging rupture, displaced kidneys, and bladder stones. Great strain is also thrown on the heart, and lung action is restricted, favoring the development of tuberculosis.

II

My first impulse was to recommend, in view of all these disturbing findings, that work benches be removed and workers told to work on their hands and knees on the floor. It would probably be wiser, however, to help them so they can know how to relieve all this strain man's evolution has placed on him. There seem to be some clear-cut and generally accepted principles which can serve as guides, in a field which has been flooded with a great deal of faddist propaganda.

Posture is an *active* thing. It is produced by the coöperation of a great number of simple nerve reflexes—although these are not yet perfectly developed in our present stage of evolution. As a result, posture needs some voluntary help since Nature is not perfectly equipped to take care of it without a little intentional assistance.

Posture is a fight against gravity. An exact percentage of good posture can be obtained by measuring length while lying down and dividing this by the length when standing up. If one habitually wins the posture fight with gravity he will be as tall standing as he is lying down.

Gravity pulls organs in the body cavity downward. If gravity rather than posture wins the fight the waist measure will be larger than the chest. Chest circumference should be 10 per cent greater than that of the belt line.

The curve should be kept in the small of the back—this can be tested readily by standing naturally with back to the wall; if posture is right the hand should fit snugly between the small of the back and the wall.

Tall, slender people should give most attention to posture as their build makes them especially prone to bad posture.

There is the kangaroo type of posture in which the upper part of the trunk is in front of the line of gravity and the legs are behind this line. The gorilla type is just the opposite. In both instances the trunk is not nicely balanced on the center of gravity, but there is a constant strain to keep the body from falling forward or backward.

III

Whether posture is "good" or "bad," there is a continual struggle of muscles to keep the body from succumbing to gravity. This may be such a habitual strain that we are not aware of it, the strain thus being doubly insidious.

Just standing may become very fatiguing for this reason. So will sitting unless mechanical support is provided by the chair to relieve the strain of the balancing muscles. When standing for a long time is absolutely necessary, the habit should be formed of carrying the body weight on the ball of the foot, rather than on heel or toe, and rests should be taken intermittently by flexing one leg and allowing the other to carry most of the body weight.

In practically all jobs, however, arrangements can be made so that work can be done either sitting or standing. Changing from the one position to the other is genuinely restful. Even office desks and chairs have been arranged so this can be done. Continuous sitting appears to be as undesirable as continuous standing.

If the sewing or assembly bench is raised about eight inches higher than is customary, and chairs made with legs correspondingly longer and provided with a foot rest, it is possible for the worker either to sit or stand and save a great deal of fatigue through these changes in his position.

Special attention should be given to the chair or stool. It should be of a height so that the sitter's feet can rest on the floor easily and squarely. When a stool is used it should be provided with a real foot rest; the rounds if used as foot rests cause the legs to be drawn back into a cramped and fatiguing position. Since people vary in leg length, the height of the chair or foot rest should be easily adjustable.

The seat of the chair or stool should be molded to fit the natural curves of the body. An ingenious efficiency engineer recently designed a model chair seat by having all his friends sit in a block of modeling wax so that he soon obtained a composite picture effect to serve as a guide. There is no particular advantage to an upholstered chair seat unless it has deep springs—which office and factory chairs seldom have. A saddle-shaped chair is better than one with an inch of upholstery. A ventilated chair seat is also to be desired.

One can sit on a soap box and conquer gravity, but with considerable effort. There should be a specially designed back rest. A rather narrow rest which will fit into the small of the back and bear gently forward is recommended. This has the same effect as when posture is measured by standing with the back to the wall and the hand passed between the wall and the small of the back. The height of this back rest should be adjustable so the chair will fit both tall and short people. The seat should be narrow enough that the sitter will be thrown back against this back rest, whether he wants to or not. The narrow width seat will make a gravity-tension-relieving posture fairly automatic.

To prevent constricting blood vessels under the knee the front edge of the seat should be gently rounded. The foot rest also helps avoid this congestion which will affect nerve as well as blood supply in a poorly designed chair and produce the effect of putting one's leg to sleep. At every point where the chair can possibly touch the person using it the corners should be rounded.

Attention to posture will not cure all the ills of man; the tense machinelike posture of the West Pointer is beautiful to watch but may be carrying the idea to extremes for the sake of military aims. But since man is built essentially as a horizontal animal, special attention is desirable for his fatigueless and efficient working in the vertical plane.

William James, the first psychologist at Harvard, observed thirty years ago that there is a redundant effect in posture, the firmly erect posture keeping up spirits, and making it difficult to entertain fears, despondency, and depressing thoughts.

PERSONAL PROGRESS POINTERS

Have I arranged my work so that both standing and sitting is possible at intervals during the day?

Do I sleep in a position that allows maximum relaxation of all muscles?

Do I have my work arranged so that I do not have to reach, or stoop, or stretch a great deal?

Is my work chair one that facilitates correct posture?

Do I stand and walk correctly?

[215]

CHAPTER XVI

GUARD YOURSELF AGAINST NOISE

I

Late in October William F. Cooper, a New York antique dealer, awoke on a Sunday morning to find a note from his wife propped up on the dining table of their apartment on East Sixty-sixth Street. Some ten years ago she had come to New York from quiet Madison, Indiana.

Seven floors below their apartment Sixty-sixth crossed Lexington Avenue, and all day and night the crazy noise of the surface cars soared upward into their otherwise cozy home. In the note she told her husband that she could not stand the eternal clanging of these cars any longer. That morning the milkman found her bruised body in the court-yard of the building, seven floors below an open window. In her hands she was still clutching a recent photograph of her husband. A tragic victim of our urban noises!

Practically every city dweller is an unwitting victim of the noises of his city. Many country dwellers are also paying a price for noise, especially those living near traffic arteries. Both peoples are struggling along trying to ignore the handicap of noise, and extreme protests such as that made by Miss Martha Bernard who came to New York from Madison, Indiana, are uncommon.

Every week I receive a few letters from people who are protesting against noise. A few of these, of course, are from cranks, but the vast majority come from highly intelligent and successful people. The president of a southern life insurance company is interested in the bearing noise may have upon insurance risks; a realtor in Buffalo is planning a new subdivision and wants to design it so noises will be kept at a low point forever, even to including some unusual restrictions in the bills of sale; a young mother in Chicago wants information to help her protect her small babe from the onslaught of city noises that bombard their apartment; an office manager of a large silverware company is seeking help in quieting some noisy machines that have taken the place of a small army of workers and are now driving the remaining workers to distraction; a young man who has inherited an old apartment building in New York asks help in protecting his tenants from the thunder of the elevated railway so he will not need to reduce rents; a street railway company in a small central western town want help in making their cars quieter so they can compete with a new bus line in attracting passengers—and so on through a most interesting and a tremendously challenging stream of letters.

I wish the copyright laws would allow me to reproduce dozens of them. They show conclusively that great numbers of our best citizens are awakening to the lurking peril of noise which has increased unchecked in our present machine civilization.

The answers I have dictated to all these are much the same: We *do* have to pay a price for noise, in an unexpected way as I will relate shortly; much of the noise of our world can be reduced remarkably, not without some expenditure, to be sure, but it is worth the outlay; and as individuals it behooves each of us to give great care to our physical and mental condition so that we can stand this onslaught. This can be done simply.

II

Before indicating the unusual way in which noise affects us, let us see what is being done to lessen noises. Mayor Price of Newton Falls, Ohio, has ordered radio loud speakers muffled after 9:30 at night—to provide better sleep for the workers of the Newton Steel Company who go to work early mornings. The sheriff of Lake County and the highway police of Cook County, both in Illinois, have started a vigorous campaign to suppress unnecessary noise of trucks —this to provide better sleep for the country folks. And a short month before this the prefect of police in Paris, France, inaugurated a campaign against the unnecessary use of the irritating tooter horn by arresting some two hundred taxicab chauffeurs the first night of the campaign. The British Medical Association agitates against noises at almost every meeting, and in America we discover the National Safety Council and the American Society of Safety Engineers maintain a joint Committee on the Elimination of Unnecessary Noise, of which I have the honor to be a member. It can be said with assurance that in a few years this will be a quieter world, and a better world for it. But in the meantime there lingers the personal duty of not only doing all one can individually to contribute to the quiet of the world, but also of taking some personal precautions so that one can resist physically the ill-effects of these noises.

III

How does noise affect people? Perhaps by causing a premature deafness, but not this way in many cases. Boilermakers do have an abnormally high amount of deafness, and Thomas A. Edison is of the opinion that the noises of civilization may induce an almost universal deafness. This is possible only if noises are increased to an impossible extent, and with the present agitation against noise it is doubtful if widespread deafness will ever occur. But there remains a more insidious effect of noise which strikes at almost every vital tissue in the body.

One point upon which psychologists are agreed is that noises of the right sort are a natural cause or stimulus of the fear reaction. Intense noises like a peal of thunder, a tire blow-out, or a revolver shot will cause a momentary and marked fear reaction in almost everyone. (The high explosives of the World War may be in part responsible for the large amount of emotional disorders among the veterans of the war, although this possibility is generally neglected in the explanations.) Considerable experimental evidence is accumulating that the more moderate noises of a modern city also cause a fear reaction, which is long continued like the noises that cause it, although it may not be as intense as the great startle precipitated by a tire blow-out. In addition to the laboratory evidence, everyone has observed that city folks living amid great noise have more driving tenseness in their behavior and have a more noticeable general apprehension than their easy-going country cousins who are living in relative quiet.

It is conceivable that if present city noises are to continue for another generation or two a typical American personality may emerge from their effects. A driving, restless, apprehensive, nervous personality—one distinctly unhealthy and undesirable, yet apparently inevitable unless the situation is promptly and frankly faced. I hope that I can arouse my readers to a full realization of the seriousness and potency of the situation which has been gradually drawing its tentacles around our civilization.

On the bodily side, we can see what is ahead more graphically. The fear reaction paralyzes the involuntary muscles of the stomach and intestines. It speeds up the heart and alters blood pressure. It increases the tonus, or tension, of the voluntary muscles. Whether awake or asleep these changes can be observed. In the sleep laboratory at Colgate University, for instance, we have seen, time after time, sleepers' blood pressure raised when a truck passes the old Colonial house used as the laboratory. Our delicate instruments have also registered increases in the muscular tension of the sleepers from such a common noise as another sleeper in the bedroom coughing.

All these changes, like those in personality traits, are of the sort of which the individual is not directly aware. Rather than lessening their damaging effects, this very fact increases them.

So when some one tells me that he has got used to noise and does not notice it any more I have to answer, "But your body has not got used to it, and your personality make-up shows many signs that you have not got used to it."

There is an interesting reason for this condition which explains why these changes brought about by noise which we cannot directly perceive ourselves are doubly insidious. Heartbeat, muscular tension, and digestive muscles are controlled by nerve centers in the spinal cord and in the base of the brain. We cannot control these in any way voluntarily or intentionally. In effect, they are what the physiologist calls reflex actions.

The brain itself determines whether or not we pay attention to a noise or notice it. So we can be ignoring a noise through preoccupation or interest in something else, but our spinal cord and brain stem will still be responding to the noise with the old fear reaction of which we are not consciously aware. Merely not noticing a noise does not mean that our body is not responding to it with continued fear reaction which may become serious in the long run.

This is something like the case of the frog who can be

placed in a jar of water over a fire, and if the temperature is raised so gradually that he may think "he is getting used to it now," soon can be boiled alive without ever protesting. His tiny brain may ignore the disturbance in his environment, but his more basic organic structure cannot withstand it.

Country girls are more buxom than city girls. And for that matter it is also recorded that country boys are larger than city boys. Why? Of course, there may be better air and food and exercise in the country. But there is also less noise. In the Colgate laboratory we are in the midst of a series of experiments which will last several years longer but which already indicate that the country quiet may be as important in this difference in general health as the country air and exercise.

We are raising cute little white rats under noise and under quiet. Both groups are getting the same food and air and light. But one brother is kept in a quiet room while the other is kept under duplicated city noises. Those kept in the comparatively quiet rooms are eating more and growing much faster than their brothers and sisters who are living under our duplicated city conditions. The "country rats" are also more active; at the end of their day they are playful and active, while their brothers and sisters who spent the day under our noises are obviously fatigued and inactive. I have had dozens of people observe the two groups of rats when there was no way for the observers to know which had been living under the noise, and without exception everyone has definitely stated that the country rats were much more active and vigorous.

IV

Since we know that the fear-reaction causes a digestive paralysis, we can now understand why the "city rats" eat less food, and why they obtain less food value from what they do eat than do their country brothers and sisters.

This may also help account for the delicatessen replacing the home kitchen in large cities.

And it emphasizes the importance of having appetizing food and the right kind of food. If anyone should give great attention and care to his diet, it is the person living or working in the midst of even moderate city noises.

On the energy-supplying side of diet we find that muscular activity, such as is present during tension, draws upon the supply of stored up glycogen in the muscles themselves. As the glycogen is used up by the muscles, a new supply has to be provided since a deficiency in this, according to Dr. Wm. R. Dunton, Jr., may cause additional fatigue. Glycogen reserves obviously should be built up by including adequate amounts of carbohydrates in the food eaten, since they are transformed by the body into glycogen later. Such carbohydrate foods are oatmeal, rice, potatoes, honey, corn, wheat, dried beans, prunes, raisins, currants.

Due to the partial paralysis of the digestive movements which propel the food in its course through the digestive apparatus being apparently decreased under the fear reaction, foods which facilitate bowel action should be wisely included in the diet also. Foods under this category are commonly called roughage foods and special items such as bran dishes. In noticeable cases the use of mineral oils or two to three heaping teaspoons of agar dissolved in water can be drunk before breakfast. Special exercises which massage the bowels also would be helpful.

Since the fear reaction also has a partially paralyzing action upon the flow of the digestive secretions, a more thorough predigestion of food by more thorough mastication can be recommended. And above all, the attempt should be made to develop a happy emotional attitude during meal time since undoubtedly this facilitates the flow of the secretions. And as far as that goes, such an attitude is excellent for combating the insidious fear reaction any time during the day.

Overfeeding, which always brings a penalty, probably brings a double penalty in cases of the fear reaction. It may be that if noise develops more in our civilization it may be advisable to eat still smaller meals, but more of them during the day. The English are doing this already in a sense, by having a light lunch with tea shortly after four o'clock afternoons, with the evening meal not ready until about eight in the evening. This is much more rational than the habit of a few Americans who take a light lunch out of the ice box just before going to bed.

Tea and coffee might be recommended on the basis of being stimulants which might produce a seminarcotic offsetting of the fatigue feelings. But in the light of the discoveries made by Dr. P. B. Hawk and his associates that these beverages apparently slow up the digestive process slightly, we must conclude otherwise. Ordinarily this might not be a matter of special concern, but in connection with the fear reaction it should be seriously weighed. Cocoa delays digestion even more markedly than does either coffee or tea. Two glasses of water rather than one cup of coffee would be a good rule.

v

How can one get away from noises? Will Hays and Arthur Brisbane work in the very top of towering skyscrapers where the street sounds become just a faint rumble. The late Joseph Pulitzer had noise-proof rooms built in his New York home and in his summer home at Bar Harbor; in addition, he had his private yacht especially fitted with silent machinery and heavy noise-absorbing rugs, and used to seek relief from the noise of the city and of his newspaper offices in the middle of the ocean.

Many people are moving into the quiet suburbs, gladly spending an hour or more a day on the railroads if only they can be assured of a quiet place in which to sleep.

Running away from danger and annoyance in this fashion does not help the great bulk of mankind, however. Most of us cannot afford the expense, and most of us cannot afford to pay the bodily and mental price noise is exacting. There is a real dilemma! There are several practical and inexpensive solutions which will make the condition of us average folks less distressing. I was talking with the medical director of a large life insurance company recently, and he told me that he keeps the radio turned on at home when the street noises become especially bothersome so that the irregular, unharmonic din is smoothed over by musical melodies. There is a vast difference in the annoying power of different noises as is being shown by experiments Ralph A. Snyder and Kenneth Coye are making in my laboratory at Colgate, and this medical director is replacing the more annoying with the pleasurable. It has long been known that music has powerful emotional effects, but not serious effects such as the fear reaction of noise.

When selecting a new home or new office, the noise of the location as well as the appearance of the place should be carefully studied. It is wise to observe the noise of the location at different times for several days, since there may be a certain hour during which it is especially noisy. It should be located at least two blocks from a highway artery. The street should be asphalt paved, and in perfect condition; brick or concrete pavements are more noisy, and even asphalt becomes a source of the most terrible noise when it is worn out—including unusually potent language at times for extra measure.

The house itself should be well built; jerry-built houses transmit noises as a sieve passes water. The windows should fit tightly to help keep outside noises outside, and also to prevent making their own rattling noise at unseemly times of the day and night. Felt or rubber weatherstripping is not only a fuel saver, but a noise and nerve saver as well. But windows must be opened at times to allow vital air to enter—what about noise then? Well, it usually comes in unchecked. But in my office at the laboratory I have special window mufflers on each window. These allow fresh air to enter unchecked and at the same time cut down the noise greatly. In my bedroom at home I have built window boxes which are lined with highly effective noise absorbing material. Neighbors can leave their radios on until early in the morning and the garbage man can make all the noise he wants to, my noise-absorbing window ventilators protect me from most of their racket. Any handyman can build such an L-shaped box lined with sound-absorbing material obtained at his lumber yard and achieve a more restful quiet.

VI

The principal secret, however, in having a restful quiet in workplaces and home is to have generous amounts of noise-absorbing materials. Rugs are excellent noise absorbers, although rugs alone will not accomplish enough. Furniture upholstered in velours, plush, or mohair will add still more absorption. Tapestries and rugs as wall decorations will add more. The greatest help in noise absorption can be accomplished by having the walls built of some of the new modern materials which absorb noise. Your nearest lumber dealer sells several varieties of inexpensive wall board. Some of these absorb noise, others do not. An architect or the lumber dealer can tell you which ones to buy for noise absorption.

I have a friend who recently finished off his attic with some of these noise-absorbing wall boards. He at once discovered that it was the quietest place in the house. Now he spends most of his time at home in the attic, and is drawing plans for a new house in which he is going to have every wall finished with this material. Ordinary plaster absorbs practically no noise. Stretching wires is of no help at all, although some buildings have had as much as five miles of wire stretched in them in the mistaken belief that this would reduce their noise.

VII

The greatest boon for the ordinary person, in addition to using all the noise-absorbing materials he can, is to discover how to relax thoroughly once or twice a day and stay relaxed for a few minutes to rest overtensed muscles. If it were a violent exercise of the muscles it would not be so serious, since their violent motion at the same time massages them, but continued tension does not have this virtue of massage.

This must be a deeper relaxation than we ordinarily think of, as has been pointed out by Dr. Edmund Jacobson of the University of Chicago in summing up his twenty years of research. This relaxation must start where we ordinarily think we are relaxed. Smaller groups of muscles, such as those in the neck, around the eyes, in the fingers, and even the toes must be intentionally relaxed in these periods, and every sensation of tenseness avoided. Of course, a quiet place is indispensable for achieving this complete relaxation.

"It is my belief," says Dr. Jacobson, "that complete relaxation periodically should have a tonic effect upon the

entire system with general elevation of health and resist-
ance to disease." In this noise-harassed generation, this
progressive relaxation should practically become a religious
observance with everyone.

How to obtain additional relaxation in unthought-of
ways has been thoroughly discussed by my old teacher, Dr.
George T. W. Patrick. "Nature has provided various
means for rest and relaxation, in sleep, play, sport, laughter,
etc.," he says. "But what will happen when the claims
made upon the working brain are in excess of the powers
of repair provided by these natural means of relaxation?"
In the craving for alcohol, tobacco, and in dancing crazes
Professor Patrick sees signs that either adequate normal
relaxation is not being secured, or that the strains due
to developments in our civilization—such as noise—are too
great to be met by our normal machinery. He would
recommend active participation in sports as a cartharsis to
relieve tension. A relaxation, but not a passive relaxation
is doubly beneficial since it is an emotional relaxation
as well. To watch a champion team on the football field
yields the spectators great emotional excitement—tension.
But actually taking part in a scrub game oneself yields
a true emotional relief from tension, in Dr. Patrick's esti-
mation. This is why schools such as Reed College, the
University of Dubuque, and Emory University have inter-
class games in which practically every student takes an
active part. And Colgate University has just purchased
a hundred additional acres of campus for use as a golf
course and for many tennis courts and other athletic purposes so that all students can get this active emotional
relaxation.

This is the paradox of relaxation through activity!

A hidden virtue in this activity itself, which aids in combating the fear reaction, is discovered in the fact that as
the muscular tension of the fear reaction draws upon the

stored glycogen it produces as a by-product lactic acid. It appears that this acid acts as a fatiguing poison until it is eliminated from the body. One of the best methods of eliminating it, according to some recent German research, is through muscular action propelling the acid along on its way out of the body just as the intestinal movements propel the food along the digestive tract. Massage of muscles helps expel this lactic acid. So also, in the light of these German experiments, does voluntary activity of the muscles themselves.

Without exception, the individual who does not obtain rather violent exercise during the regular course of his daily occupation should see that he obtains exercises in stretching, lifting, pulling, and throwing, which exercise even vestigial muscles. As is evident from the preceding paragraph, exercises in which groups of muscles are twisted slightly so as to enhance the massaging effect will probably be most helpful in this connection. Care should also be taken that every muscle gets some stretching and twisting; the fear reaction undoubtedly affects practically every muscle in the body and formal exercises which involve principally the trunk, legs, and arms produce only half results from this viewpoint. Head twisting exercises the physical instructor sometimes is criticized for using may thus be more vital than a tiring period on the bars.

In my office in the Colgate Psychological Laboratory I have taken special precautions to keep noise from becoming bothersome. The ceiling is covered with sound-absorbing acousti-celotex. Velour drapes are on the three deep windows and a davenport upon which I relax on occasions is upholstered in velours. At the windows are window mufflers which allow fresh air to enter while keeping most of the noise outside.

When I feel fatigued from too long sedentary concentration on the details or data of an experiment, I will either relax for a few minutes on the davenport, with my eyes loosely closed, or else I will obtain relief from the fatigue sensations by going into the adjoining room which is a small carpenter shop, and there saw and pound in a half hour of semistrenuous physical exercise combined with making coarser apparatus. It so happens that my job is such that I can get this relaxation while exercising and still be productive on my job—something like the salesman who travels from office to office. Often I do rough carpenter work that the janitor should do, but if he did I might be cheating myself of the stretching, cramping, stooping, twisting, and hammering that helps keep one in trim for guarding himself physically against the invisible demon which has crept over our world: that blanket of noise which precipitates a fear reaction whether we want it to or not.

PERSONAL PROGRESS POINTERS

Do I have my work and sleeping rooms generously supplied with materials that absorb sound?

What am I doing that unwittingly and needlessly adds to the noise of the community?

What annoying noises in my working environment could be lessened or completely removed?

Can I concentrate on work if necessary when noise is bothersome?

"Never say an ill thing of a person when a good thing can be said; not only speak charitably, but feel so."

—Rule adopted at age 18 by *Elizabeth Fry*, who became the famous Quaker prison reformer.

CHAPTER XVII

I

SLEEP comes so naturally to one that he seldom realizes that there is art even to sleeping. Some realize this, however, and we find Edison saying that no healthy person requires more than two hours of sleep a day. Such men as Humboldt slept only three hours a day while John Hunter slept only from three to four hours a day.

What would happen to you if you were to try sleeping only a certain number of hours each day? Perhaps, if you really understood the hygiene of sleep, you could cut down your sleeping time considerably.

We sleep deepest during the first hour or two. The muscles are most relaxed then, the blood pressure lowest, and the skin sensitivity lowest. This is the time for housebreakers to prowl since one is harder to awaken during the early part of sleep.

Sleeping late mornings is not so restful as the early sleep soon after retiring. It may be more restful than no sleep but it is not deep and recuperative sleep.

You can get along with less sleep if you take a nap after the noonday meal. It is sometimes maintained that half an hour of sleep after lunch is equal to three or four hours of sleep just before arising in the morning. Many of the eminent persons who obtain only three or four hours sleep daily make this possible by taking one or two short naps during the day.

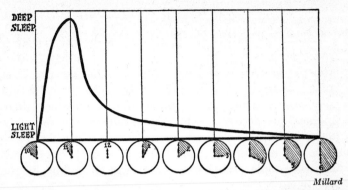

Millard

THE HEIGHT OF THE CURVE SHOWS HOW DEEPLY ONE SLEEPS EACH HOUR
OF THE NIGHT. LATE MORNING SLEEP IS NOT THE MOST RESTFUL

I know of many persons who have tried these naps with
great success. It is hard the first few days to be able to
go to sleep immediately and to refrain from sleeping several
hours after once asleep. Sleep habits can be formed,
though, just as any habits and, after a short time, you
can go to sleep at once and awaken almost at the moment
desired. These naps should be followed by a short period
of exercise, such as rapid walking, to help shake up the
food in the digestive tract.

II

Eating solid food before retiring is harmful because the
usual bodily activity of walking is absent and the food
is not propelled along the digestive tube. The bad dreams
one has after eating before retiring may not be due to the
food that is eaten. As a rule, these dreams are the indirect
result of the excitement that is usually present at parties
where food is served. Coffee is sometimes blamed for keeping persons awake but, in many cases, the restlessness is
caused by the excitement.

[231]

III

You do not need to be tired to go to sleep if you know how. Sleep is not invariably a result of fatigue. More often, it protects you from fatigue. One goes to sleep before his work has harmed his body, thus protecting the body from fatigue. As a matter of fact, extreme fatigue is oftentimes accompanied by sleeplessness. Infants sleep longer and deeper than adults, and one would not think of an infant as fatigued. Old folks, also, sleep longer than business people even though they may do nothing to tire themselves.

You can understand why old folks sleep longer, and how to go to sleep better when the two prime factors back of sleep are considered. These are *muscular relaxation and monotony.*

The donkey sleeps standing up. Human beings seldom attempt anything like that. Still, I knew a man several years ago who slept standing up in his bed. For several weeks I observed him. All night long he would stand there, never once losing his balance. After a few weeks, he began to sleep again as most human beings do.

There must have been something wrong with this man, you are probably thinking. There was. When I knew him, he was a patient in a hospital for mental afflictions. That is about where all of us would be committed if we tried sleeping the way he did.

This man is an extreme case, but he illustrates well the point that I wish to make: how you sleep has much to do with your mental efficiency. Not everyone sleeps in such a tiresome way as this man did, but few people know the most restful way of sleeping.

He was violating one of the prime conditions of restful sleep. That is *muscular relaxation.* You can fight off sleep by clenching the fist, or by holding your muscles

[232]

taut. You can coax sleep by relaxing every muscle in your body. Muscular relaxation not only hurries sleep but it makes it more restful.

You can improve your sleep habits by beginning tonight to relax carefully every muscle in your body after you are in bed. Relax the arms, legs, trunk and neck muscles. Do not sleep in a cramped up position. Your dog can teach you a lesson in this particular. Try waking him when he is sleeping curled up with his muscles taut. Then try it sometime when you find him stretched out limp. It will be much harder to awaken him in the second instance. He is sleeping more soundly and getting better sleep because all of his muscles are relaxed.

IV

The other requisite for sleep is monotony. Excitement prevents sleep. Old folks sleep so much largely because their existence is monotonous. Country folks may sleep longer than city folks, not because of more work, but because of more monotony.

Monotony may be produced in several ways. Some years ago, a boy was found who had all his senses paralyzed except one eye and one ear. When a bandage was put over his eye and his ear packed with cotton, he promptly fell asleep because he had been deprived of his main sensory impressions. We can secure monotony by sleeping in a quiet room. That is not always possible, however. But we do not have to hunt for quiet to find monotony. It is found in regularly repeated sounds, such as the continual clank-clank of Pullman wheels over the rail joints, or the incessant tick-tock of a clock in the bedroom. The rocking of the cradle and the "sing-song" of a mother's lullaby produce the same effect on a baby.

You will sleep better if you can avoid all noises in your

sleeping room. One can sleep inside a boiler factory if he knows how, but it is not restful sleep. It has been found that the passing of a trolley or a motor car beneath one's bedroom window while he is sleeping raises the blood pressure immediately, although the person may not show any other signs of awakening.

We need comfortable sleeping arrangements in order to obtain relaxation and monotony. Physical comfort is necessary to eliminate all sensations of discomfort. Muscular relaxation is largely dependent upon bodily comfort. The pillow raises your head slightly and keeps the blood from rushing to your head.

V

Which would be more fatal, to go without sleep or without food? Both are uncomfortable enough. Experiments on dogs have shown that insomnia is more often fatal than loss of food. Starvation could be carried until the animals had lost half of their weight, and still they would recover when again fed. Starvation could be kept up for twenty days, but five days loss of sleep proved fatal!

But sleeplessness is oftentimes a gift, not an affliction. Of course, loss of sleep is harmful but the fact remains that, in ninety-nine cases out of one hundred, sleeplessness is a gift rather than a disease. This does not lessen the gravity of the effects produced by the loss of sleep. They are present and cannot be forgotten. But this statement should alter one's attitude toward insomnia.

The perfectly respectable woman with apparently orderly habits who complains that she has not slept for the last week would no doubt greatly resent being classed with the drunkard who has been on a spree for the same period of time. Psychologically, however, they are both pretty much the same. The one has been indulging in strong liquors; the other has been indulging in sleeplessness.

One of the best remedies for insomnia is to know that in the great majority of cases it is an indulgence. The effects brought about by this indulgence are not the evidence of some severe underlying disturbance. They are merely the results of a mental dissipation that is akin to any other kind of dissipation.

If sleeplessness were a disease, there would be just cause for alarm. But who has ever heard of sleeplessness getting the best of anyone? The drunkard does not stay on his spree perpetually. He takes time to recuperate between sprees. The same conditions holds true for these "going without sleep" sprees. Little permanent harm is done. The person with insomnia "sobers off" at times long enough for his body to get back into a healthy state.

The difficulty is to get the mind back into a normal, healthy-minded attitude toward sleeplessness. The mental causes back of sleeplessness are many and varied. The person so troubled seldom realizes what is the basis for his peculiar attitude toward sleep and the habit of sleeplessness that he develops. They have their origin in the mental underworld in most cases. Going without sleep is a good way to gain attention that is unconsciously wanted. Loud clothes, long testimonials at prayer meetings, vague aches and pains are other means of obtaining, somewhat unwittingly, this desired attention. So with insomnia. It makes an interesting conversational topic and gains for one an undeserved sympathy and position of prominence. Did you ever know of a person bothered (they were really blessed!) with insomnia who did not always inform his friends just how much sleep he had lost during the last three weeks?

Worry commonly accompanies insomnia. It is not the cause of the sleeplessness, however. Going without sleep gives good cause for worry. The person who has little else

[235]

to worry about and still craves to do so may develop insomnia so as to have something to fret about.

Insomnia is pernicious, but it is also a gift. By slight warps in human nature, some people come to like such pernicious things for the unwitting gratification that they bring. They have attitudes that are far from healthy-minded. A reliable prescription for breaking up a case of insomnia is to refrain from talking about it, worry about the high cost of living in place of how awful insomnia is, and work enough during the day so that sleep will come as a refreshing tonic.

VI

It is astonishing to know how great the restorative powers of good, sound sleep are. Some sleep is not as refreshing as other sleep; but even poor sleep is better than none.

Experiments on the mental effects of loss of sleep show how great a restorative sleep is in accelerating mental functions. Memory tests in the case of one man, whose initials were G.N.B., took 134 seconds before the start of the loss of sleep. After going without sleep almost four days, he was unable to memorize any of the parts of this test. Loss of sleep had played havoc with his memory abilities.

The four days without sleep were followed by a period of deep, refreshing sleep. Only a third of the four nights of sleep that G.N.B. had lost was made up. Here is what shows the great restorative powers of sleep. After he had slept, he was able to memorize a similar test in 106 seconds. This was an improvement of 28 seconds!

Arithmetical abilities, such as those involved in addition, are also affected. Problems that took 120 seconds to add at the beginning of the experiment required 130 seconds at the end of four days without sleep. But, again, after a third of the lost sleep had been made up, similar problems could be solved correctly in 109 seconds.

VII

To obtain the most mental and physical benefit from sleep one should move into a quiet neighborhood where trains, trolleys, and taxis will not change the blood pressure or increase the tension of muscles. Although we may be unconscious of these alterations in our vital adjustments there is much evidence that we pay a price for them. How a more restful quiet can be introduced into the sleeping chamber was shown in the chapter on noise. Practice that, too.

VIII

What kind of a bed you sleep in is also important. When on a hunting trip you may be able to sleep soundly on the hard, damp ground. But ordinarily you are not so doggedly tired as after a hunting trip and should watch your sleeping equipment closely.

If you have a lumpy mattress throw it away. Sleep in a bed at least 39 inches wide, so you can turn during the night without being half-awakened with a fear of falling out. Sleep alone, so movements of the other sleeper do not disturb you. Have the head of the bed placed so that early sunrise or lights from passing cars do not fall on your eyelids.

Do not use a bed that has springs that sag at your hips. A cheap spring almost always sags, regardless of what the salesman tells you. A spring made of a large number of vertically placed coils is the best since it allows for the surface conforming to the shape of the body surface. (See the chapter on posture again in this connection.)

If you use a mattress which has springs built into it, in winter it would be wise to place a warm blanket under the bottom sheet, since these inner spring mattresses are cold. In cold weather, also, wool or camel's hair blankets should be used since they have the greatest warmth with the least weight on the body. A soft and pliable blanket is the best since it naturally hugs the body and keeps it warmer than a starchy blanket. Blankets which are extra wide are warmest, since they hang over the edge of the bed and prevent cold draughts. John Wanamaker shrewdly observed in this connection that "the part of the bed clothes that keep us warm is the part that hangs over the bed." Oversize sheets also facilitate sleep comfort since they can be tucked far under the mattress and will not loosen and become tangled as the sleeper turns over during the night.

It is not known what effect, if any, colored sheets have on sleep.

Avoid a combination of spring and mattress that has "side sway." It should give just up and down and not sideways.

A bed can be too soft for best sleep. These are very comfortable to recline on, but the sleeper's body is buried so deeply in them that it is necessary to wake up to turn over. Ordinarily one turns many times during the night without knowing it; in a too soft bed one has either to stay in the same position, which seems to be against nature, or he has to wake up to turn, which also seems to be against nature.

IX

Most sleeplessness is caused by worry or imagination. Or, in some people, it gives them something to talk about.

If a physician is giving you a medicine or hypodermics to help you sleep, the chances are that he is giving you some entirely neutral mixture and that it is your imagination that makes you sleep afterwards. Human beings are that way. But if it is excitement or worry and not one of these queer quirks that is keeping you awake, try the following:

Take a neutral bath with the water at a temperature of 92 to 97 degrees Fahrenheit (use a thermometer). Stay in the tub for fifteen minutes to half an hour.

If you are physically very tired out and not excited, try a hot bath for perhaps ten minutes, keeping the water temperature at about 97 to 100 degrees.

X

Habits of sleep are important. You should have regular hours for retiring and for rising. If you know you are going to be out late one night, sleep more than usual the night before, or take a nap the afternoon before. That is what the veteran banquetgoer, Chauncey Depew, did.

Above all make certain that you have conditions and habits of adequate sleep. If you need an alarm clock in order to get you up on time, the chances are that you are starving yourself on sleep.

XI

Some people believe that sleep is just a bad habit, acquired before there were electric lights to make the night beautiful and interesting. I have even been misquoted as stating such an absurd idea.

If sleep is a habit, it certainly is not a bad habit, but a very beneficial one. A race which does without sleep is well on the road to becoming a race of mentally disordered people, probably within the first generation. Sleep

[239]

is not merely a great restorative, but its dreams are often a safety valve for sanity. So if a pill ever appears which is alleged to make sleep unnecessary I would warn you still to take no substitute for sleep, real sleep and plenty of it, under the best of conditions, and dream pleasantly to your heart's content.

PERSONAL PROGRESS POINTERS

How can I arrange my routine so that I can take a half-hour nap after the noon meal?

Do I tell others how poorly I have slept?

Do I enjoy telling them?

Do I get enough physical exercise to be tired when bed time arrives?

How can I lessen the distractions present while I am sleeping?

"It is always legitimate to rise above one's self, never above others."

—Maxim by *Julia Ward Howe,* adopted during the strain of the War Between the States, shortly after she had written "The Battle Hymn of the Republic."

Now we will complete the circle. The book started
with a study of the general environment. Then we
studied you and me. We have left the important
topic of the *intimate environment* in which you and
I live and rest, play and study, rejoice and grieve—
OUR HOME.

CHAPTER XVIII

A HOME FOR EFFECTIVE LIVING

I

MANY persons are uncomfortable in the presence of a
psychologist because they feel either that their thoughts
are being read, or that they are being diagnosed as a moron.

Not content with making everyone generally uncomfortable, these fiendish psychologists are now making their
thrusts at the houses we live in. They are finding that
some houses which are tremendously expensive are morons.
They are also finding that some small cottages rate as a
genius on the psychological scale for measuring houses.

Everyone will be more comfortable when builders and
architects plan houses in accordance with these psychological pointers, so perhaps psychologists may be forgiven for
making people mentally uncomfortable by diagnosing
everyone they meet.

To *reduce fatigue* to the lowest possible minimum is one
aspect of psychological engineering in the home. This depends partly upon how the floor plans are arranged, partly
upon how the furniture and working equipment is distributed throughout the house, and partly upon the planned
thoughtfulness with which the housewife does her work.

Does your house cause you unnecessary steps due to the
way in which the rooms, or linen closets, or switches are

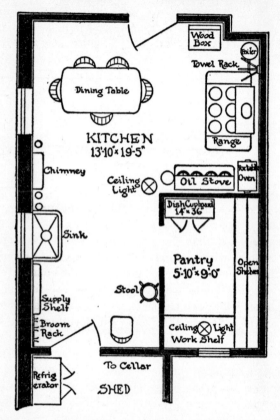

THE ORIGINAL FARMHOUSE KITCHEN

There are many suggestions for the psychological betterment of the workplace of the home in these two kitchens. The second plan brought about a saving of 1 hour and 40 minutes in the time spent in kitchen work each day. Here are the stages by which this tremendous saving was accomplished: Adding a stack table saved 139 steps. Putting a drain board at the sink saved 234 more steps. Adopting a wheel tray to transport things from one place to another in more

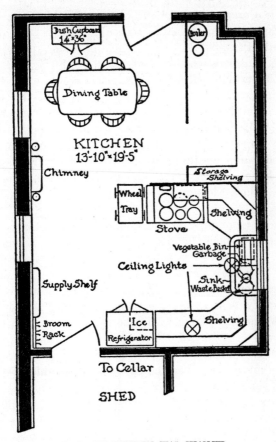

Dish Cupboard 14"x36"

Dining Table

Broiler

KITCHEN
13'-10" x 19'-5"

Storage Shelving

Chimney

Wheel Tray

Shelving

Stove

Vegetable Bin

Garbage

Ceiling Lights

Sink-Waste Basket

Supply Shelf

Shelving

Broom Rack

Ice Refrigerator

To Cellar

SHED

HOW THE KITCHEN WAS CHANGED

than handful lots saved 389 more steps. Rearranging the utensils saved another 168 steps. Rearranging the supply of foods saved 218. Making the whole layout more compact saved 154 steps. An electric mixer saved 9 steps. Other minor changes brought the total saving to 1,385 steps. (Courtesy Vermont Agricultural Experiment Station; work of Marianne Muse.)

placed? Can you prepare a meal for a family of five without leaving a swivel stool placed in the center of the kitchen? Perhaps your arrangement of rooms and working utensils causes fatigue, unnecessary steps, lifting and moving which a more effective arrangement would eliminate.

Obviously a big house is more tiring on the housewife than a small house. A small kitchen with shelf-cupboards on the walls and a space for the ice box is less fatiguing than a large kitchen with a pantry on one side and an enclosed porch on the other in which the refrigerator is kept. High shelves which require stretching, and low shelves which demand stooping add to the burden of fatigue.

Filigree trimmings on the woodwork, and French doors help make a house a moron by adding to cleaning difficulties.

The telephone should be placed only after thoughtful consideration. The housewife will walk many unnecessary miles every year unless the phone has been placed equidistant from the places where she is usually at work. Ordinarily a convenience, the telephone can readily become a nuisance by thoughtless placing. I have plugs in every room in my house—even the bath—so a portable telephone can be plugged in wherever I am working or resting.

With a house perfectly laid out from the psychologist's viewpoint, the working habits of the housewife may still generate almost inconceivable amounts of fatigue. Some housewives are famous, almost notorious, as fussy busybodies who are always hard at work and yet accomplish very little. Duplicate dust cloths placed on the second floor will relieve the busybody of some unnecessary trips up and down stairs.

Stew pans and kettles into which water is drawn in preparing a meal should be placed within easy reach of the water tap. Then many steps each day will be saved since the utensils can be grasped and filled with the necessary water without having to take a step. Vegetables such as potatoes should also be kept within easy reach of the sink so that they can be picked up, pared, and washed without having to take a step or having to stoop.

The coffee canister and the empty pot also belong within easy reach of the sink without taking a step to keep the kitchen from becoming a moron.

There are many insidious sources of fatigue in the house. Take the way beds are placed in the bedrooms, for instance. They should be placed so that the sun or early daylight does not strike the sleeper's eyes; otherwise they make the last hour or two of sleep less refreshing, and the new day may be started before one has fully recovered from the fatigue of the previous day.

Noises are also an insidious source of fatigue. This is especially true of noises which will disturb one's sleep without awakening him. A bedroom facing away from the street is often the best sleeping room since many disturbing and fatiguing street noises are thus avoided. We shall learn much more about this soon.

II

To *avoid all possible embarrassment* is another phase of psychological engineering applied to a home.

In those modest days before short skirts, hot air registers used to cause considerable embarrassment. A house with large archways between rooms may give an air of grandeur, but it does not allow adequate privacy to avoid all possible embarrassment. Noisy bath fixtures and poor wall construction which does not prevent the transmission of noise is a potent cause of embarrassment day in and day out.

The stairway to the second floor should be placed so that when the minister comes the man of the house can go upstairs from the basement workshop to clean up without being seen from the living room.

We have already mentioned the telephone; it may also cause embarrassment if the conversation is overheard by guests, or even other members of the family. It should be placed in a closet or nook so that conversation cannot be overheard. This is not adequate protection on party lines, however, when all the neighbors lift their receivers and listen in on the conversations every time the phone rings.

Bed room lights should be placed near the windows so no revealing shadows can be projected on to the window shades when retiring.

A small hamper for soiled clothes should be in each bed room to prevent embarrassment from clothes scattered about the room. There should be a decorative waste basket in all other rooms of the house to catch scraps and waste the minute they are formed and give the house a perpetual ship-shape appearance which will avoid much embarrassment.

Bungalows appear to be the home of most embarrassments. A second floor is highly desirable to give privacy.

III

To *avoid all possible annoyance* is another phase of making the house psychologically right.

Poorly built houses with windows and doors that stick are the source of much mental irritation and annoyance. So are loose windows that rattle in the least gale. And water taps that drip, drip, drip all day and night.

Small water pipes that lessen the flow of hot water in the bath mixture when hot water is drawn in the kitchen sink come under this classification—although perhaps they might come under the next as it has happened that small children have been seriously scalded by the temperature of their bath water changing when cold water was drawn to sprinkle the lawn.

To spend ten minutes hunting for a favorite paper or deck of cards is annoying and could readily be saved if a definite place were allotted for these commonly used items. All members of the family should be thoroughly trained in replacing these in their exact niche.

Electric light switches are especially potent at causing annoyance. This is principally because they are usually hard to find at night. The worst offender is the pull chain switch fastened right at the fixture with a small button dangling in the middle of the room. Try to find it at night and still keep your temper!

There are numerous small items used daily which could be purchased in duplicate, or even quadruplicate, to save much annoyance. There are ash trays, for instance. The annoyance of having to hunt all over the house for one, or the worse annoyance of letting ashes fall on the floor, can be saved if they are generously sprinkled throughout the house. Pencils, too, should be given the same liberal treatment.

One housewife told me that the most annoying thing in the world was to prepare to start a hurried meal, only to discover that there was not a match to be found. It developed that she bought one box at a time. For one dollar one can buy a hundred and twenty boxes of safety matches and eliminate two or three last minute purchases of single boxes during an ordinary week.

And what about creaky floors, and tree branches which the wind scrapes back and forth across the roof—not to mention an unsoldered electrical connection which flashes the lights off and on?

IV

To make every home *free from all accident hazards* is a fourth phase of using psychology to have more comfortable homes.

[247]

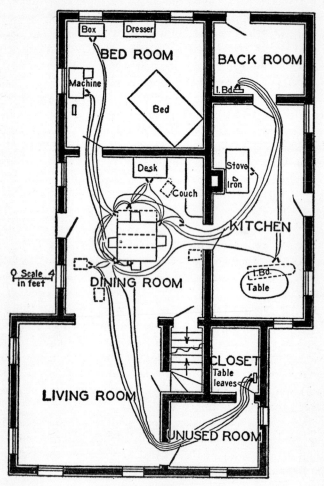

THE ORIGINAL SEWING PLAN

The housewife may save money by sewing at home, but usually she does not save herself. On the left we see traced the steps taken by one woman in making an apron in assembling the material, doing the really productive work, and later putting away the extra table leaves, iron, and such. A home-made cabinet, about the size of a wardrobe cabinet was put in the bed room to house all the items used in sewing, even including a special lightweight folding table for

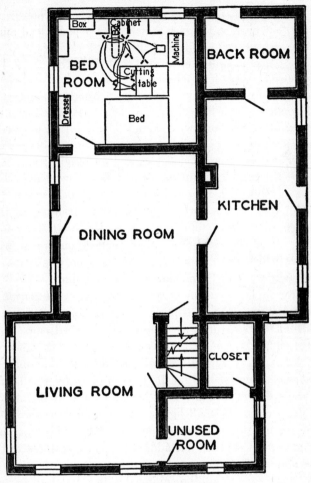

THE NEW ARRANGEMENT

cutting and basting; this is shown on the right. The original plan required walking 524 feet to make the apron. The rearranged plan required only 40 feet of walking. Similar thoughtful planning will make great savings in most house work. (Courtesy Cornell University Agricultural Experiment Station; work of Ella Cushman.)

Mark Twain suggested that going to bed was a dangerous thing to do, since most people died there. There is no
humor, however, in the fact that home accidents lead automobile and factory accidents.

This phase is subtly connected with the other three, but
is important enough in its own right to be given independent emphasis. If fatigue has not been brought to the van-
ishing point, for instance, the accident hazard is increased
because the tired housewife cannot be careful. Under adequate annoyance, also, the irritable husband may lose his
temper and suffer an accident caused by blind fury.

Falls are prominent among serious home accidents. Did
you ever slip on a rug? Not on a large rug, or a heavy
rug, for their weight and size gives enough friction traction
to keep them from slipping on even the most hazardous
floor. It is the small rugs that connect one room with
another which are the principal offenders on this score.

Slippery rugs are a menace to life and limb, as well as
a source of embarrassment and annoyance. As a rule it
is not the rug that is slippery but the floor. Rubber or
linoleum floors are not as slippery as polished oak. Part
of the difficulty can be taken care of at the rug, however.

A large heavy rug will not slip as readily as a small or
light one. Rugs should not be held in place by small nails
or brads driven into the floor because these in themselves
are dangerous. If small light rugs are used it seems wisest
to use some non-slip mat under the rug. This not only
prevents most slipping but adds a luxurious softness to the
rugs and lessens wear.

All stairways should be equipped with a handrail to provide safety. Unusual turns in stairways are another hazard. Small rugs which lie loosely at the tops of stairways
are to be severely condemned.

High shelving in closets and cupboards is to be avoided

on two scores—it induces the strain fatigue due to stretching, and it precipitates many falls.

Talk with any man six feet tall about the basement of
his house. Prepare yourself for strong language before you
ask him, however, for it is probable in nine cases out of
ten that he has battered his head against a water or heat
pipe in the cellar on the average of once a week for years.
The extravagance of digging a deeper excavation can be
spared and yet not have a low bridge effect in the basement by a careful routing of the obstructing pipes along
side walls where they cannot batter out gray matter.

Cellar steps usually appear to be an after thought, or
perhaps they are devised by the devil himself. Narrow,
winding, and dark they are the dimly illumined scene of
much domestic disaster. To complicate matters further
many housewives, driven to desperation over the lack of
adequate closet space, drive oversize spikes into the walls
of the basement stairway to catch on apron pockets, ears,
and eyes.

Snowy weather brings a treacherous slipperiness to the
porch steps. There are special slip-proof treads which can
be used to overcome the hazard of a rude reception to some
visitor who may bump himself uncomfortably on several
of the steps in one spectacular fall. Rock salt or ashes or
sand can also be used in season.

The flush plates on electric switches should be of rubber
or other insulation to prevent the danger of shocks which
are always present with the metal flush plates.

At once a menace and bother, safety razor blades also
present one of the hardest problems to solve. Several serious accidents can be traced to these. A friend of mine in
Utica, who had previously taken the psychologically perfect house idea as a joke has an entirely changed attitude
about this work the past three weeks, all on account of a
razor blade.

He was called to a late Sunday morning breakfast. Only partly awake, he was hurrying to wash. He took the cake of soap, wet his hands, and started to rub the soap over his hands, changing it from one to the other. Suddenly he noticed that his hands were bloody. A razor blade had been carelessly placed in the soap dish the night before and had stuck to the bottom of the wet soap. In soaping his hands the keen edge had cut several serious gashes in his hands. A dozen stitches had to be taken in each hand, and he was kept from work the greater part of a week.

Whether new or discarded, these dangerous blades present a real problem. They present a hazard even when thrown in the ashes or garbage. They must be completely destroyed. This demands either that they be melted in the furnace fire box, or dissolved chemically.

A temporary compromise can be reached with these keen-edged demons by buying a child's small bank at the five and ten cent store and burning both blades and bank when it is full.

v

This new application of psychology demands a broadened conception of house building. The structural engineer comes into the picture in the specifications of materials to give most satisfactory wear under years of weather strain. His job is largely to guide economical spending in the purchase of materials, oftentimes by recommending a slightly more expensive material which will stand up under years of service better and be less expensive in the long run.

The psychological engineer has the difficult task of correlating all the elements of the building so they revolve around the dominant features—the human beings who will live in the house. The materials engineer's field is to relate the properties of the various materials to certain building stresses and strains. The psychological engineer's field is to relate materials and forms to human stresses and strains, as we have briefly illustrated.

A house becomes a home, it has been said, when it is designed to live in. This should be amended to specify effective living. And one cannot live effectively even in a palace if it is arranged and used to cause any avoidable fatigue, embarrassment, annoyance, or accident.

Designing and constructing a house to be a genius on a psychological test, however, does not assure in any sense that after people have moved into the house it will still retain its originally high rating. Thoughtless use and poor arrangement of kitchen tables and other details of equipment may render it a moron on this new mental test.

There are many houses which held their heads high when they were completed but through ill-considered use they now bear the stamp of a moron.

VI

*One hundred and one ways to tell whether your house is a moron.**

Is Your House a Moron?

Each question answered "Yes" is favorable, while a "No" answer is unfavorable.

1. Does the outside main entrance lead into a vestibule or hall instead of a living room?
2. Is the stairway to the second floor accessible without passing thru rooms on the first floor?
3. Are the dining room and living room so situated that an unexpected caller seated in the living room can not watch the progress of a meal in the dining room?
4. Can one enter the bathroom without passing thru

other rooms or being seen by persons in other rooms?

5. Is the bathroom constructed to prevent the transmission of noises?

6. Are there opaque shades on all windows which prevent silhouettes of persons inside being seen when the room is lighted?

7. Can all doors be opened irrespective of the position of any other door?

8. Are all doors so arranged that when opened they do not cut down light from the windows?

9. Is the water heating system such that hot water can be obtained almost immediately when a faucet is opened?

10. Are all bells non-starting?

11. Are the house numerals in a place where they can be readily seen both day and night?

12. Is there a roomy clothes closet at the front entrance for storing coats and rubbers?

13. Is each bedroom provided with a roomy clothes closet?

14. Are electric switches placed so that it is not necessary to walk into a dark room in search of them?

15. Is the telephone so placed that one's conversation is private?

16. Are the kitchen shelves so arranged that the contents of the highest and the lowest shelf can be reached without stretching or low bending?

17. Can mail be left inside the house by use of slot or small opening?

18. Can refuse and garbage be disposed of without the use of an unsanitary outside receptacle (by means of incinerator, etc.)?

19. Is the house planned and constructed so that noise transmission from one room to other points of the house is practically eliminated?

20. Are all rooms free from slanting ceilings?

21. Can all door locks be opened by a single master key?

22. Are there lights with conveniently located switches in all closets?

23. Is the house situated in a quiet place?

24. Is there toe room under all cupboards in the kitchen?

25. Is the house of fireproof construction?

26. Are the floors slip-proof?
27. Is there a safety handrail beside the bath tub?
28. Do all the rugs lie flat and stationary on the floor?
29. Are all steps seven and a half inches high and nine inches deep?
30. Are all staircases straight?
31. Are all staircases provided with handrails at a convenient height?
32. Are the cellar ceiling and pipes high enough to make stooping unnecessary?
33. Are the door knobs set in far enough to prevent bruising knuckles on the door frame when closing?
34. Are radiators shielded so as to prevent burning one's self?
35. Is there freedom from the danger of ice and snow falling from the roof in the path of persons below?
36. Is there a safe and convenient means for disposing of safety razor blades, toothpaste tubes, etc.?
37. Is there a fire screen covering the entire front of the fireplace?
38. Are all walks even and level?
39. Does the kitchen adjoin the dining room?
40. Are the kitchen furnishings so arranged in relation to each other (i.e., distance from stove to sink, etc.) that needless steps and waste motions are eliminated?
41. Is the telephone centrally located?
42. Is fuel stored conveniently near the heating plants (i.e., fireplace, furnace, etc.)?
43. Is the dish cupboard accessible from both dining room and kitchen?
44. Is there a lavatory and toilet on the first floor?
45. Is there a bedroom on the first floor?
46. Is there a clothes chute from the second floor?
47. Can kitchen utensils be placed or stored where they are used, so that they can be grasped without unnecessary motions and effort?
48. Are the work tables, benches and sink in the kitchen at such a height that when standing erect with arms hanging loosely in front of him and with palms up, one's knuckles just touch the work surface?

49. Is there a stool which can be used while working in the kitchen?

50. Are outlets for electrical appliances which are used intermittently (such as electric iron, vacuum cleaner, etc.) waist high so that stooping is unnecessary in connecting up the appliances?

51. Can radiators or heat registers be turned off easily without stooping?

52. Are the mop boards free of square corners which are difficult to clean?

53. Are the contents of cupboards visible thru glass doors?

54. Is the color and pattern on the wall pleasant to the eye?

55. Is there a thermostat regulating the heating system?

56. Can the rooms be lighted artificially without glare or gloom?

57. Is the house illuminated in daytime without glare or gloom? (Doors should not shut out light from windows when opened. Strong light should be diffused by curtains, especially in the case of a window over the kitchen sink. There should be at least one window in small rooms and two or more in larger rooms.)

58. Does the vestibule or hall provide room for receiving salesmen or callers with whom one is not intimate?

59. Are floors free from all gratings of heating systems, to avoid embarrassing air currents from the floor and to eliminate the liability of small articles being lost?

60. Are cooking odors from the kitchen kept from escaping to other parts of the house?

61. Can one enter the first floor bathroom without being seen from the living room?

62. Is there a shelter for visitors waiting for you to answer the bell?

63. Is there an outside receptacle for groceries?

64. Are all water pipes laid in inside walls so that they do not freeze in winter?

65. Are pilot lights (small bulbs which indicate whether or not another light is on) provided for lights which can not be seen from the main rooms of the house?

66. Are the rooms on the same floor on the same level?

67. Is there a light at the front entrance to the house?

68. Is there a convenient outside access to the place of fuel storage (such as coal bin, oil tank, etc.)?

69. Are bell buttons, knockers, etc., in a conspicuous place?

70. Are all water faucets turned on in the same direction and with a single turn?

71. Are all hanging lighting fixtures at least seven feet high?

72. Are there outside water faucets which are conveniently located?

73. Is the bathroom adequately ventilated by means of a window, fan or other special arrangements?

74. Is the water from the refrigerator drained off by means of a pipe leading to the regular drain?

75. Are all electric motors for refrigerators, oil-burning furnaces, thermostatic heat control, etc., insulated against noise and vibration transmission?

76. Can water be drawn at all outlets with equal pressure, regardless of the flow at other outlets?

77. Are all pipes run between walls?

78. Is there a safe and easy access to the attic?

79. Can one readily see who is waiting for admittance before opening the door?

80. Without trying the door, is it possible to tell by some indicator whether the bathroom is occupied or vacant?

81. Are there either casters or "Domes of Silence" on all movable furniture?

82. Do living rooms have sufficient wall space for tapestries, paintings, etc., for artistic effect?

83. Are the gutters and leader pipes large enough to take away the water or melting snow as fast as it collects on the roof, to prevent water from backing up and spoiling interior walls?

84. Are the roofs and outer walls insulated to prevent the admission or escape of heat?

85. Can the bedrooms be entered without passing thru other rooms?

86. Are screens tight fitting and yet easily removable without leaving a marred window-case?

87. Are all faucets of the combined hot and cold mixing type?

88. Is all the woodwork of plain trim to avoid unnecessary dust collection?
89. Are the windows of the sun room equipped with glass that admits the health-giving ultra-violet rays from the sun?
90. Are lavatory waste devices of the "pop-up" type rather than the chain and plug style?
91. Are there adequate facilities for laundry work (i.e., stationary tubs, washing machine, steady table-height ironing board, place to hang out clothes)?
92. Is there a swinging door with a small glass window between the kitchen and the dining room?
93. Is there a convenient place for storing brooms, vaccuum cleaner, and other cleaning utensils?
94. Are all bells audible in all parts of the house?
95. Is there a warm place to dress in the morning?
96. Are the door knobs of such a shape that they can be easily grasped and turned even when the hands are wet?
97. Is there an outside entrance to the cellar?
98. Is all equipment (such as door knobs, plumbing fixtures, window frames, door frames, etc.) of standard size and style?
99. Are all wires leading into the house underground?
100. Can all meters be read from the outside of the house?
101. Is the general outline of the home of nearly square shape?

"You should go through life doing what you believe to be right and not bother yourself over what people might say. They will soon forget their criticisms."

—Advice given by *Abraham Lincoln* to a young man in his twenties, *A. B. Farquhar*, who became a large manufacturer of farm implements.

CHAPTER XIX

I

You have to be a psychologist as well as an electrical engineer to know how to use electricity properly in the home. You have to be an electrical engineer to know whether your wiring system will safely carry the load a new labor saving appliance will draw through your house wires. Electrical engineers, for instance, tell me that the average house wired five years ago is a potential fire hazard since the increasing use of household appliances has overloaded many old wiring plans to the point where they are in almost daily danger of breaking down.

A coffee percolator and toaster draw the equivalent of about one horse-power of electricity. In many homes this horse-power is taken out of a flexible green cord hanging in the center of the kitchen; the cord being originally planned for a 60 watt bulb, while now 1,000 watts are being drawn through it when these two appliances are used together to prepare an easy breakfast. We'll learn more about this kitchen cord shortly.

The psychologist comes into the picture in such a case as this because the worry and apprehension about household fires is widespread and in many instances is due to a suspicion that the wiring system of the house is old, too old to be trustworthy. Electricity itself is a mysterious matter to most persons—including electrical engineers and physicists—and this very mystery adds to its force as a cause of worry. A good investment in worry prevention is to have the house rewired, using sealed metal conduit tubes for the wires so there is absolutely no danger of fire from hidden sources. This is often a good cash investment since it may reduce insurance premiums, but if you ever have an evening spoiled by wondering if there is a fire at home it is worthwhile purely from the psychological standpoint.

II

A remarkable thing, which I am at a loss to explain, is why many homes have wall switches for all electric lights except the one in the kitchen. The psychological rule is that there should be a switch conveniently placed just inside the door of each room. And this goes for the kitchen, too.

Some rooms have two entering doors. In this event it will pay in mental composure in the long run if there is a switch placed at each door, wired as when a switch is placed at the top and bottom of a stairway. This makes it possible to switch on the lights at once before a dark room is explored, and on leaving the room at the other door the lights are left on until the last instant.

I have lived in houses where all wall switches had been placed approximately in the center of the house, since that could be done with least expense. There was as much stumbling around and irritating fumbling as if there had been swinging cords in the center of the room to search out. This arrangement, far from being a saving, is a total loss since it is no improvement upon the much cheaper system of no switches at all.

In our work in the psychological laboratory we have studied the psychology of various types of switches. You would be surprised to know the variety available. And some of them are really wonderful machines. Such a one is a mechanical marvel which will turn on one bulb the first poke, two bulbs when punched the second time, three on the third push, and so on. To turn on a light in the room and then turn it out again requires five punches on the hard rubber knob. A mechanical marvel, but a mental nuisance!

The snap switch we have found undesirable since it requires an awkward, wrenching, twisting rotation of the wrist which is as tiring as using a screw-driver. The type of wall switch with a white button to turn the lights on and a black one to turn them off is an advance over the snap switch, but still not the psychologically best of the assortment we have examined.

The tumbler switch has come on to the market within recent years. This has a black rubber stump projecting from the wall. When turned one way the lights go on, when turned the other way they go off. This seems psychologically best since it is not necessary to locate the exact button as it is with the other types. A simple swing of the arm over the section of the wall where the switch is known to be will actuate this tumbler type and have the lights turned on before the button could be located with the other types, saving time as well as annoyance.

It is especially desirable that all switches throughout the house and garage be uniform so that a single switch habit can be formed and all lights turned on without thought or fumbling. A house with a push button switch for the living room, snap switch for the dining room, tumbler switch for the cellar light, and a swinging green cord for the kitchen is very unpsychological in these details. Even the switch at the head of the bed for the bedside lamp should be uniform with the wall switches, and, incidentally, should also be a wall switch to thwart the near-heart failure caused about once every three years by knocking down the bedside light when feeling around for the switch on it.

III

Electric typewriters are difficult to sell because many stenographers share the householder's unwarranted fear of electricity. Although a speedier and easier machine to operate, many are afraid that it will shock them. Perhaps they have had unexpected and painful experiences with switches or irons that make them feel that way. All danger of shocks can be removed from switches if the flush plate is hard rubber or bakelite. If you do not have these, include them in your next specifications, and in the meanwhile if you ever receive a shock from the present equipment call in an electrician at once to run down the trouble.

Plugging in vacuum cleaners, irons, and other conveniences are the principal sources of "shock anxiety." This can be entirely eliminated. As a rule this shock anxiety is justified. Floor plugs a few years ago were just modified sockets and the plugs had to be screwed in. If a finger were accidentally inserted into the plug one's rheumatism was given an unexpected electrical treatment. When we were living in Iowa my son was nearly electrocuted when he was visiting an elderly lady who told him stories. In creeping across the floor he saw a screw-in plug receptacle, investigated it with his hands, and was knocked unconscious.

Invention has supplied the modern plug which has only rubber exposed with two tiny crevices to receive the copper prongs from the sweeper, and psychological sense recommends only this type of plug. Even when this is used there is still a lurking hazard if the machine is disconnected by pulling the wires, which tends to loosen the wires inside the plug cap and may precipitate a short-circuit with resulting

[262]

sparking and sputtering. The plug should always be removed by pulling the hard rubber cap, not the wires. Recently there appeared new inventions which fasten around this rather inconvenient cap and supplies two good handles with which it can be pulled from the receptacle; there are also plugs with a neat handle for grasping as an integral part of their structure.

IV

Plugs used for floor and desk lamps should probably be located in the mopboard for appearance. Convenience plugs used for sweepers and such, however, should be about waist high so that stooping is avoided. These can be hidden from view if they are placed as close as possible to the window frame so the drapes or curtains conceal the plug. It is essential to eliminate all possible stooping for it is hard work. If the housewife were forced to lift a hundred pound weight from the floor she would rebel at the task as unreasonable. Yet every time she stoops she has to lift a hundred or so pounds of her weight back into standing position, and that is avoided by having the convenience outlets waist high.

Wall switches which control the ceiling lights are usually placed too high. Children should be considered in the wiring of a house. The switches should be compromised between the best height for an adult and the best height for a pre-school child. If the tumbler type of switch is used this will not lessen their convenience for the grown person.

When conveniences are used psychology can also be applied to advantage. The loose section of the cord from the electric iron, for instance should be kept out of the way while ironing by having a string and screen door spring fastened together to hold the loose cord out of the way and keep it from becoming entangled. The vacuum sweeper should be pushed more slowly than it usually is to save housewife's fatigue and do a better job of cleaning. The door bell should be tuned by placing folded paper behind the gong so that it is not startling as most bells are. (For the last four years we have been using a bell with a gong removed; this produces a pleasing, soft hum.)

The scientific use of electricity to save eye strain was briefly mentioned in the second chapter. This is so vital in planning a place to live that it deserves a special chapter to which we turn now.

> "The President, the Cabinet, and Congress to boot can't enact poor men into rich. Hard knocks, and plenty of them, can only build up a fellow."
>
> —Observation of *David Crockett*, frontiersman who became a congressman and was killed in the battle of the Alamo.

CHAPTER XX

I

MAN's great superiority over animals is due to the more facile use of his brain, his hands, and—his eyes.

When Standard Oil displaced candles in home illumination eye strain was greatly reduced. Electricity made available lighting appliances for further elimination of eye fatigue. Proposals seem to have been made just as well— if not better—under candle light as under the glare of electricity.

With the advent of electricity, however, such great power was placed at the householders' disposal for lighting that many have overdone it and actually placed a needless burden upon their eyes.

The selection of wall covers and room colors must also be given careful study by the householder who is aware of the value of the eyes and the importance of giving these delicate cameras every protection. But more about these after we find out about the right use of light to save eye strain and oftentimes subsequent headaches and general tiredness.

There are some people who seem to believe that a single electric bulb can perform a miracle and expect it to light an entire room. Of course a large bulb can make an average room brilliant with light—but that is not adequate lighting since the high powered bulb causes glare fatigue of the eyes. It is much like looking at the bright sun for a few seconds.

Of the two evils—high intensity lighting which produces glare, and dim lighting without glare—dim lighting is the better, but even that is subjecting the eyes to a continual strain. The dim light places most of its strain on the delicate automatic lens just behind the pupil at the front of the eye, while the glaring lighting fatigues the sensitive nerve cells near the back of the eye ball. Too bright light may actually destroy these receptive nerve cells. That is why forest rangers in the Rockies always wear dark colored goggles when they are out of doors and the snow reflects the glaring sunlight into their eyes.

A 75 watt bulb hanging on a two or three foot cord in the center of the kitchen produces glare—unless it is properly shaded. Yet to be able to see into the kitchen sink when she is washing dishes in her own shadow the housewife often has even a larger light bulb placed on this cord. Now, 75 watts is not adequate for the average kitchen, and yet glare can be avoided by a little simple engineering. The neighborhood electrician, or perhaps the handyman around the house, can place a 40 watt bulb over the stove tight up to the ceiling, a 60 watt bulb over the sink and tight to the ceiling, 25 watt bulb where it will shine into the ice box, and another 60 watt bulb in the center of the kitchen and hugging the ceiling.

This illustrates several important principles to be followed in checking up on what can be done to the house lighting to save eyes. First, it is better to *have the light come from small bulbs scattered around the room* rather than from a single large bulb. This makes the lighting more uniform, avoiding dark corners, and eliminates much glare. In the living room of my home, for instance, there was just a large central fixture when we moved in. We now light the room with small bulbs in this fixture and seven small wall, floor, table, and bridge lamps each with a frosted bulb.

Then, second, *the bulbs should be arranged so they cannot be seen.* This further eliminates glare. In the kitchen we suggested that they be placed tight to the ceiling, since that would usually keep them from being seen directly by the eye except in the case of large kitchens. In the other rooms of the house study should be made of shades. Shades with an opening in the top need to be placed on lamps which are arranged so that light coming through the opening does not strike the eyes of anyone sitting or standing in the room. Yet it is not unusual to see a small shade originally intended for a tiny bulb used with a large bulb, the most of which sticks up through the top of the shade. Careful shopping for better shades and discarding some old shades for a rummage sale of curios will work wonders with many tired feelings.

That *most rooms need more artificial light than they enjoy,* is a third principle. A conservative rule is that there should be from three to four watts for every square foot of floor space in the room. If the room has high ceilings there should be proportionately more electricity used in lighting. Also, if the wall color is dark more watts should be used. A heavy colored, opaque lamp shade, for instance, cuts down the lighting efficiency of a bulb. The sand colored shades are effective in letting the light from the bulb out into the general room.

Tin shades should be thrown into the basket with the empty tin cans. Green glass along with them. They are a poor attempt to correct for having a strong bulb hanging in front of one's eyes.

II

Scattering light by numerous small lamps with well chosen shades not merely saves eye fatigue, but it also gives an opportunity for clever and effective decorating with light. As a rule rooms are decorated solely for day-time effect, while at night their entire appearance may be changed by the arrangement of lights.

Take green colored shades to illustrate the point. I am sure that this has a deterrent effect upon proposals—unlike candle light and Standard Oil. Green colored light—and blue is a similar sinner—produces a ghastly, super-human effect. Lips lose their natural color and rosy cheeks appear ashen under these rays. Green and blue are usually considered cool or calming colors and their use is to be recommended on summer draperies and slip covers—but do not let these two colors predominate, or even appear, in the lighting scheme of a room for their ghostly pall is anything but calming.

At the state hospital at Moline, Illinois, they have some rooms decorated entirely in green into which they move mental patients who have become excited. Other rooms are decorated entirely in red and patients who begin to feel mournful and depressed are transferred to these rooms. This is a different matter, however, from having a colored light or shade which casts its colored pall over a room and its occupants. It can be worked out in wall coverings, drapes, upholstery, and rugs. A reddish tinged window drape for the winter months and a greenish tinged one for summer is a capital application of this principle.

The predominating color of human beings is reddish, and they show up to best advantage in a light with a slight tinge of this color. Yellow and reddish lights, also, are least fatiguing on the human eye, next to white light. These hues should be favored in the selection of shades.

III

Just as a shade may cut down light, so can wall color. Many rooms are dimly lighted even in broad sunlight because of deeply colored somber walls which soak up the light like a greedy sponge. Of course heavy velour or lined drapes which extend over half of the window may also cut down the light; these should be kept pulled well back away from the window. But the wall color itself has a powerful effect on total lighting of a room.

Ceilings should be white to reflect all possible light downward, with the effect of expensive indirect light which is the best. In case the ceiling is papered it could be re-papered to advantage once a year without disturbing the side walls. This is important since the collection of invisible and unremovable dust greatly lessens the lighting value of a white ceiling. In case of painted ceilings, a magnesium rather than a lead paint should be used. This is slightly more expensive, but maintains its high light reflecting power for many years longer than the lead paint.

For the side walls, light colored papers and tints are to be given preference. Reds and yellows can be recommended for their eye saving qualities, but it should be a light pink and a light buff that is used, not a deep red such as used to be on hotel furniture and railroad coaches.

IV

The effect of lights depreciates rapidly. Unless they are carefully dusted it is easily possible for them to lose ten per cent of their lighting power in a month. All bulbs should be cleaned regularly with a clean, damp cloth about every alternate week. Care should be exercised that the cloth is not wet enough to drip water into the socket, since this may blow a fuse or begin corrosion in the socket. With a damp cloth there is no danger. In this respect numerous wall and table lamps have another advantage over ceiling lighting since they can be reached more conveniently for regular cleansing. In many factories they have

[269]

crews of men who do nothing but clean electric bulbs, year in and year out.

v

In planning a new home provisions should be made for an ample supply of convenient outlets. There should be a convenience outlet on each wall, and on walls with windows they can be installed to advantage near each window, since people are most likely to be sitting there.

It costs only a few pennies more to have a double convenience outlet installed where a single one had been planned. This makes it possible to plug in a vacuum sweeper without having to remove a light plug. It will also save expense in the long run since sooner or later the light plug which was removed is stepped on and broken.

How Different Wall and Ceiling Colors Help Lighting

color	percentage of light it reflects
white—new	82-89
white—old	75-85
cream	62-80
buff	49-66
ivory	73-78
light green	48-75
dark green	11-25
light blue	34-61
pink	36-61
dark red	13-30
yellow	61-75
dark tan	30-46
natural wood brown	17-29
light wood varnished	42-49

The value of grays varies remarkably, ranging from 17 to 63, depending upon how the paint is mixed.

And a word if there are elderly persons in the home. With advancing years "stronger" eye-glasses and brighter light are necessary. Grandmother may need a larger light bulb!

CHAPTER XXI

THE PSYCHOLOGY OF HOME HEATING

I

THE average home in England is kept at a lower temperature than most American homes. Which is the wiser? Let's see ——

One of the most marvelous of the phenomena of mother nature is the way the human body maintains a uniform temperature of 98.6 degrees regardless of the temperature of the surrounding air. It is a living miracle. Only when disease germs or something else serious goes wrong inside does the body change from its fixed temperature.

Why worry about room temperature then? Indeed we should worry about the temperature outside of the body, as we saw earlier, for it throws a strain on the body functions that regulate this internal precision in heat if the room temperature varies much either way from 68 degrees! That is, unless some precautions are taken, but that is getting a bit ahead of the story.

The mental man as well as the physical man is upset when this optimum outside temperature is not available. Assault and battery cases increase, disciplining school children increases, factory accidents are more numerous, and working efficiency is lowered when the mercury goes either above or below 68 degrees.

My observations are that the average American home is kept too warm in winter. So my first recommendation, that you keep your home cooler in the winter, may put money into your pocket *via* the coal bin by keeping closer to a temperature of 68 degrees.

It may be necessary, however, to spend some small change to be safely comfortable at this temperature. American homes are usually kept too warm either because cold air leaks into the edges of the room and has to be offset by greater heat on the interior hallways, or because poor designing of the heat or steam lines demands that most of the rooms be overheated in order to allow one or two rooms to be warmed at all. The first can be overcome by using felt, metal, or rubber weather-stripping around windows and doors; by storm windows and storm doors; and by having the outside walls of the home so that they are of a heat insulating construction. Jerry built houses will inevitably have to be heated to around 80 degrees at their center to take the chill off on the outer sides of rooms.

Adding a section or two to a radiator in a room that is difficult to heat, or installing a larger hot air pipe, will often bring the temperature of the average room down nearer to the desirable point of 68 degrees. Weather-stripping and heat insulating will, of course, also help avoid the one or two cold rooms to be found in most homes.

II

Too much emphasis cannot be given to the tremendous importance of keeping the winter temperature in each room in which people live within a degree or two of 68 degrees. A thermostatic control of the furnace drafts makes this partly automatic. But this will not insure a uniform temperature in all rooms, since the controlling thermometer may be located in a warm or cold spot in the house. If they can be afforded it is a wise investment to have a thermostatic valve at each radiator which will automatically turn it off or on depending upon the temperature in that particular room, not upon the temperature in a downstairs hall where the controls of furnace drafts are located.

The cheapest way out of this dilemma is to have a thermometer in each room, located either on the warmest or coolest wall. One of the best habits to which children can be trained is to keep close watch of these thermometers in winter. Adults can form the same habit with profit, too. The temperature should be regulated in individual rooms first by opening or closing the radiators, not by opening the windows to melt the snow outside.

These thermometers are apt to be a "false alarm," however, unless fairly good ones are purchased. If you will study the temperature on the showcase in a store where a dozen cheap thermometers are displayed you may be amazed to discover that one thermometer says it is as much as ten degrees warmer than one beside it. Investing two or three dollars in a *good thermometer* will pay dividends in health and efficiency—if the warning is heeded when the winter mercury reaches 68 degrees. The thermometer must give a fairly exact reading since the optimum, or critical, temperature of 68 degrees is not simply an approximation but has been arrived at with a great amount of precision.

In our sleep laboratory at Colgate, for instance, we record the temperature of the sleeping chambers of our experimental subjects with a thermometer costing almost two hundred dollars. I am not recommending such a super-accurate instrument for each room in your house, but get a good one. There are jerry thermometers just as there are jerry built houses. You usually get what you pay for —and it is a Scotchman who writes that. But that is getting away from the story.

III

If you will pardon me again, I'll inject another personal item. Some time ago I moved into a new place with steam heat. Since I knew that a uniform temperature of 68 degrees was not the whole story, important as it is, I jimmied each of the radiators slightly. I did this because moist air is desirable. The average home is actually drier than the Sahara Desert in winter. Hot water or steam heating does not make the home any damper since the steam or vapor is tightly sealed up within pipes. But by adding a small petcock to each radiator and keeping these slightly open a tiny jet of steam played into the room continually and noiselessly, adding to the humidity of the air in which I lived.

The water pan which is hooked back of some radiators does not help the humidity as much as this simple contraption any plumber can install for a small charge. One serious fault with the evaporation pan on top or behind the radiator is that nine-tenths of the time it is dry as a bone. They are useless unless they are kept filled with water. They can be purchased with an automatic float connected to the water supply system which keeps the pan filled without watching. These, obviously, are much more expensive than the simple petcock, but this fails in the case of hot water heating systems. Your plumber will know whether this can be used or not.

To the man of the house who has faithfully poured a gallon of water into a little pan on the side of the hot air furnace every morning I would say that he might just as well have rubbed a rabbit's foot and looked at the moon over his right shoulder. It is true that most of this water evaporates and is carried through the heat pipes into the rooms, but not enough can be evaporated by this method to accomplish an iota of good. Continuous and automatic sprays can be introduced into the cold air intake, however, and upwards of a hundred gallons of water evaporated in a day or two. This helps.

Dampness in the basement is not hazardous because of it making the house damp; the trouble is that this can serve as a breeding place for bacteria and foul odors. While it may contribute slightly to the humidity in the house, which is desirable, it is to be condemned because of its menace to health and well being. Years ago there was an excuse for damp basements, but with the present development of construction knowledge the correct use of waterproofing cements will make the new basement watertight, or the old basement can be treated to overcome its faults.

Temperature can be readily and cheaply controlled—in fact it can be controlled at a cash saving every year. Humidity is also important, but it is more difficult to control, although any house can be made right in humidity for around two hundred dollars. In the long run this expenditure is likely to be saved in furniture not coming unglued and growing squeaks, and by rugs wearing better. It will also save the startling little electric shock received after walking across a dry rug.

IV

When we consider what to do to keep the temperature at the psychologically correct point in the summer we find revealed the cooling power of air in motion. Temperature, humidity, and air in motion make up the triumvirate of guards we have available to lessen fatigue and disease and irritability through temperature control.

The temperature outside as I am writing this is just above 90 degrees; inside it is 75 degrees. This great reduction has been accomplished by heat insulated walls, and by keeping the window shades on the sunny side of the house drawn, and all the doors and windows tightly closed to prevent the hot outside air from entering.

But even 75 degrees is too hot to be comfortable or efficient, even though it may be a triumph of good building and common sense that it is no hotter than that inside. The third musketeer—air in motion—saves the day. Ever since I took my first course in applied psychology I have always kept my summers productive by turning on an electric fan at the first sign of discomfort from the heat. Air heated to 75 degrees but kept in motion has the cooling power of air many degrees colder.

Southern mansions are built with a long hallway across the entire first floor which acts as a natural flue for the circulation of moving air.

On hot nights for years we have slept with an electric fan directed toward the wall so that the direct breeze does not chill, and with the noise muffled by having a good fan and further standing it on several layers of sound-absorbing felt. An oscillating fan is most desirable for preventing continued direct drafts.

Last summer when motoring west during the hot part of the year we carefully packed an electric fan and on stopping for the nights were careful to stay only places with electric current so the fan could be used, and that was the first thing unpacked. While others were sweltering and complaining under the heat, our old friend air in motion kept me in good enough condition to write a year's series of articles for which I had just contracted.

Keep the temperature down, the humidity up, and in hot weather keep the air on the move!

v

The frog and the alligator are poikilothermic—their body temperature changes to correspond with that of the outside air. Man does not have this feature that takes a word of fourteen letters to describe. It taxes his constitution to maintain a uniform bodily temperature under the vicissitudes of room and outdoor temperature.

Keep the temperature down, the humidity up, and the air in motion!

CHAPTER XXII

HOW TO LET THE SUNSHINE IN

I

Do you remember how grandmother used to keep the window shades tightly drawn in the musty "front parlor." She wanted to keep the pitiless sunshine from bleaching the dyes in the floor coverings and curtains.

Today her grand-daughter knows no fear of fading dyes, thanks to modern dye chemistry. So the shades are up all day long, and possibly far into the night. She is letting the light in without much restriction, but she is not letting the sunshine in. Her windows skim the sunshine, allowing the light to enter the rooms but holding the health-giving rays of the sun outside as effectively as though the window opening were covered with a sheet of lead.

Children who live in the house will be prone to develop rickets, tooth decay, sallow complexions, tuberculosis. Children who live on the other side of the windows will be relatively free from these unpleasant conditions.

There are miracle working powers in sunshine which are denied admission through our ordinary windows. These powers are worth going outside to get, or bringing inside through special windows.

Closely related to the deep purples and violets we sense, are the sun's rays which are called the ultra-violet. These are invisible to the human eye. They are the miracle working short rays. Civilization is robbing us of these— but inventive science is returning them to us rapidly.

Clothing, houses, smoke polluted atmosphere all conspire to keep the ultra-violet rays from striking the surface of our bodies.

First science found a substitute for sunshine which would do part of the work Nature has depended upon sunshine doing for years. Physicians had long known that cod liver oil was a good "tonic" for use in run-down conditions and nearly a specific cure for rickets, although its potency in curing the twisted bone developments of rickets has been definitely known only for recent years. Sunshine and cod liver oil and halibut liver oil will work wonders in rickets, but children prefer to take the sunshine.

The anti-rachitic properties of cod liver oil have long been attributed to Vitamin D, but now sunshine is known to produce a Vitamin D effect. It is as though we were to take our medicine without touching a spoonful.

This revolutionary discovery is of great significance to the home-maker. Complexions, "pep," tooth decay, healthful children, and tuberculosis are all involved in the practical applications. Two definite things are indicated. The most obvious is to get into the open sunshine as much as possible; the second is to design and redesign our homes so that sunshine will get in—not just light, but actually sunshine loaded with ultra-violet rays.

We will dismiss the matter of getting into the sunshine outdoors and see what can be done within the home itself.

II

A family friend is an expert research scientist, but without children of her own. Two years ago she was chosen god-mother for her newly arrived niece. Taking her responsibility as god-mother seriously she promptly arranged to present her niece with special windows for her nursery to allow the sun's rays to enter without having the cream skimmed off and left outside. A far-sighted gift which promised both health and appearance.

Railroad coaches in England are already being provided with special glass for their windows so that the traveler will not be given skimmed sunshine. This sensible practice was started by a railroad taking passengers to the Cornish Riviera at the extreme south of England. Most of the passengers on this train are going to the Cornwall coast to get away from fog-ridden smoky cities and to soak up some complete sunshine laden with the ultra-violet. But the practice has extended in England, where, I believe, they are more awake to the value of ultra-violet in late years than most Americans are.

Ordinary window glass is a complete barrier to ultra-violet rays. Fused and glass-clear quartz will let the rays through almost perfectly. For a few years fused quartz, developed by Dr. Elihu Thomson, was the only way known to allow ultra-violet through a substance which could also serve as a window pane. Despite the fact that it cost around $100 a square foot it has been used widely, and in the home of the National Vaudeville Artists quartz has been used for roofing some rooms.

While quartz is one of the most perfect transmitters of ultra-violet known, it is ruled out of use in homes because of its cost and also because it is usually full of tiny bubbles which hamper vision.

More recently less expensive and more serviceable window glass has been developed which will allow about 50% of the ultra-violet to pass through into the room. When the ultra-violet transmitting glass is first manufactured it will usually allow much more of these priceless rays to pass, but after a year or two of aging its efficiency is cut down somewhat. It looks like ordinary window glass, and is only slightly more expensive. Half a dozen manufacturers are now making glasses of this variety.

I have known of two or three instances where new houses were fitted with ultra-violet glass throughout. This is a somewhat unnecessary procedure. It cannot let ultra-violet rays through where there are none. Only windows which are struck by the sun need to be fitted with this newer glass.

To vary the phrasing a bit: All windows which are struck by the sun's rays should be fitted with an ultra-violet glass.

And one should sit in these windows in the sun as much as possible—but be careful not to overdo this on a bright day at first for you may be sun-burned! The vitalizing powers of these glasses was first discovered in 1901 when workers became severely sunburned.

In mid-summer there are about ten hours of sunshine a day. In mid-winter there are only about four hours. Spring fever is now considered to be due in a large portion to the deficiency of ultra-violet received during the winter months. Such being the case, the right sort of window glass is a spring fever preventative. And we can now understand how the grandfolks were helped by generous spoonsful of cod liver oil in the spring-time.

III

Mid-winter vacations to Bermuda and to the West Indies have taken the place of cod liver oil among those who can afford it.

But I know a hard-working executive who is too busy to take a vacation in mid-winter. He has solved the problem of ultra-violet aid, however, by having a second small office which opens from his private office. This smaller inner office is fitted like any office with telephone and dictaphone, but in addition there is a nickel plated stand holding a precious quartz tube which will make an intense ultra-violet at the touch of a switch. He spends fifteen minutes in there on each of two days every week, getting in effect the sunshine benefits of a two weeks' vacation every week.

I make use of an ultra-violet lamp regularly myself. Ordinarily these should be used only under the direction of an expert. There is a definite dosage which should not be exceeded; if it is painful burning may result. There are certain periods when women should not receive these more concentrated ultra-violet rays. For increasing the brief four hours of sunshine each winter day, and for a safe-guard against a cloudy week which skims away the ultra-violet such lamps are highly useful. The cheaper machines which are sold for a few dollars across bargain counters usually do not produce ultra-violet rays at all. They give a purplish colored light and tickle the skin, but that is all.

I would urge the purchase of an ultra-violet lamp for every home, in addition to fitting appropriate windows with transmitting glass; but buy only a lamp which is rec-ommended by your physician or by some impartial expert, and use it only under their general advice as to dosage.

Some progressive public schools now have rooms fitted with these lamps where the children disport themselves with a minimum of clothing each week under the super-vision of the health department. Such "sunshine rooms" are especially to be desired in schools which serve the crowded sections of our large cities.

IV

The problem of adequate ultra-violet is especially press-ing in cities. The smoke haze skims away some of the ultra-violet before it reaches the tops of the skyscrapers. Then the tall buildings cast shadows hours long upon their neighbors across the street and still further restrict the ultra-violet rays. The set-back construction now demanded in the larger places will help lessen the shadows, but will not provide window glass which will give what ultra-violet is outside free access.

A scientific confrere who resides in New York City lives in an apartment more expensive than he can afford, but does so intentionally to obtain ultra-violet. It looks over Central Park, thus avoiding a building across the street which might cut off the ultra-violet supply. In addition a large three-sided bay window hangs slightly over the street, giving sunshine a window through which it can enter morning, noon, and afternoon. These, of course, are fitted with glass which does not skim off the ultra-violet rays. While this is an ideal situation for anyone, it is esecially desirable in the present instance since it has enabled him to combat tuberculosis successfully and still keep at his work. For days at a time he could be seen semi-nude, working busily in the ultra-violet bathed bay which actually saved his life.

v

Some day we may no longer be dependent upon the sun for ultra-violet benefits, but that day is in the future a considerable distance. It has been found that many food articles can be treated, or irradiated, with ultra-violet so that they take on added virtue. They taste the same after being irradiated, but treat the body better. Almost any food except those which are already spoiled can be irradiated and thereby benefited. Powdered milk was one of the first foods to be treated this way.

The foods so treated do not store up the rays themselves, but seem to be modified chemically so that they contain ergosterol after the irradiation of the proper dosage under an ultra-violet lamp.

There are three definite ways known in which the body is helped to health and beauty through the aid of ultra-violet. These rays kill bacteria on the surface of the body, or very near the surface, in a very few seconds. As a second definite aid they cause an increased flow of blood to the parts which receive the rays, and thus benefit from the nourishing and disease-combating virtues of the blood. As the third definite aid it now appears that they change some of the surface fats of the body into ergosterol, and ergosterol produces the same results as vitamin D, if, indeed, it is not actually this elusive vitamin.

Whether we eat irradiated foods, or whether we have windows that transmit the ultra-violet into our homes, we can at least throw our ordinary windows open on mild and sunny days and get some of the benefits which have been stored in complete sunshine for us.

"Light is the very life-blood of Nature," says Sir David Brewster. Get all of it you can into your home,—complete light, not skimmed light.

"Save half of what you earn; look ahead; and hang on—never let go."

—Advice of Donald Smith, Scotch boy who moved to Canada where he developed the country's resources, became the first *Baron Strathcona and Mount Royal.*

CHAPTER XXIII

QUIET COMFORT IN THE HOME

I

Two years ago a new house in a southern city was awarded a prize in a national architectural competition. Two weeks ago the owner of that house wrote me for help on making the house quiet. And the best advice was to sell it! The location of the house was such that to have made it quiet enough for living purposes would have entailed heavy expenses.

It is much more economical and effective to design the house from the start so it will be quiet, rather than to attempt to engineer quiet into it later. But it is never too late.

A sensible freedom from disturbing noise is desirable, not just because it gives the home an air of luxury—it is practically imperative for resting tensed nerves and preventing an insidious form of fatigue which follows in the wake of noise.

There should be a sensible freedom from noise in every home, not a dead silence which may be more disturbing to some persons than rank noises. The truth is that most houses err in being too noisy,—I only know of one house that is said to be too quiet, and that was built by a man who is somewhat over-enthusiastic about noise control and absorption.

II

Care and foresight in considering outside noises in selecting the site will simplify the problems of making the house quieter. A trolley car makes around 60 noise units. (Zero is just inaudible, 100 intense enough to make the ear drum tingle.) Work in our laboratory reveals that with an intensity above 50 there is a drain on bodily energy due to noise being a natural stimulus to cause the fear reaction.

By considering the noisiness of the location much later trouble can be avoided. Trolley and truck routes should be kept three or four blocks away from the site. Brick or cobblestone paving should be avoided since they add to traffic din. A hillside site with a steep grade is undesirable due to screeching of brakes when cars are descending, and whirr of gears of up-going cars. Tall buildings nearby or houses constructed close together also make the neighborhood rate worse on the noise score, for they restrict the open air which is a perfect absorber of sound energy.

III

Most houses heated with a hot air plant have an effective loudspeaker system in the air ducts. In a house we recently lived in it was possible to sit in the kitchen and hear the conversation in the front living room at the other end of the house, three rooms away. This explains why some of my friends think I can read thoughts!

Steam or hot water pipes can also be good conveyors of noise, but there are on the market joints which prevent much of the transmission of noise through these media. The annoying thumping of water-logged heat pipes is a sign of poor plumbing.

The most prolific source of noise embarrassment is from

the bathroom. Often this is due to ill-wisdom in the location of the room. When placed in a jog of the downstairs hall the entire hallway serves as a noise amplifier, distributing it to all parts of the house. Great care should be exercised in placing the downstairs bath to see that its sounds will not be broadcast.

Special wall construction should be used around the bath to prevent the transmission of noise through the partitions. A double partition is to be recommended, and should be thoroughly sound insulated at all points of contact.

The bathroom door should be fitted tightly to jambs which are lined with felt weather stripping to prevent leakage of noise. A key hole, ridiculous as it may seem, should also be avoided for enough noise can easily filter through such a small opening as to offset expensive engineering precautions, although it should not be implied that noise insulation of the bath is expensive. There are on the market doors which have absorbing material between their panels and which lock around the rim after the fashion of a safe door when the knob is closed These are highly effective, and if they can be afforded should be installed on all sleeping and bathrooms. Otherwise felt stripping of the jambs of these rooms should be closely adhered to.

IV

There are two principles which will be of most helpfulness to the home-owner or builder in conquering the very real menace of noise The first is that partitions, including floors, ceiling, and windows and doors, should be constructed to prevent the transmission of much noise. The second guiding principle in the conquest of home noise is that furnishings and wall coverings should be selected to yield as much noise absorption as possible.

Here are some of the many practical applications of the first principles:

How Different Partition Constructions Affect the Transmission of Noise from One Room to Another

(Data from Dr. Paul E. Sabine, Riverbank Laboratories, Geneva, Ill.)

Partition construction	Average reduction factor*
4" hollow clay tile, plastered on both sides	3.36
2" gypsum tile, plastered on both sides	2.95
1½" solid metal lath and plaster	2.53
2 × 4" studs, wood lath and plaster	2.73
2 × 4" studs, sound absorbing wall board with coefficient of .20 used as base for plaster on each side	3.02
2 × 2" double studs, staggered, sound absorbing wall board with coefficient of .20 used as plaster base on each side, and extra sheet hanging loose between the studs	4.32

* The higher the average reduction factor the more sound proof the partition.

Outside noises, which are the chief source of trouble, filter readily into the house around loose windows and doors. Felt or metal weatherstripping should be included in the specifications of every home to save both noise and coal. As much as fifteen per cent of the noise in a house can be eliminated under many everyday conditions by keeping the windows protected. While weatherstripping interior doors may not save coal, it is valuable to look after this detail to prevent the embarrassment of private conversations being overheard.

Heavy and rugged partitions and walls stop more noise than those erected by a jerry builder. So-called deadening paper which comes in rolls has but slight effect in preventing the transmission of noise. There are now on the market several forms of bona fide noise and heat insulating materials which can economically and sensibly replace deadening paper. Some of these are made from tough sugar cane fibers, some from flax straw, some as a packing house by-product in the form of felt. Some of these can successfully be used as a plaster base.

The home builder should carefully examine into these materials and make a thoughtful selection of those with most heat and noise insulating utility. The engineering departments of any of the firms can supply you with facts about these properties of their material.

A rule without many exceptions is that material which is heat insulating is also noise insulating. Used just under the outside siding, and also on the other side of the studding as a plaster base, noise transmission will be greatly lessened as well as the coal bill.

V

A house built in the vicinity of heavy traffic presents difficulties. The very foundations themselves may transmit so much noise as to offset careful wall construction to avoid noise.

In a Connecticut city, for instance, a house half a mile from a railroad and in a quiet locality had the reputation of being haunted. The ghost was finally discovered—by geologists who found that the house foundations rested on a great sheet of rock which appeared as an outcropping half a mile away immediately under the railroad tracks. When a heavy train passed its rumble and clank was actually telegraphed through the rock strata and shook this particular house while those on either side of it were undisturbed.

The use of steel cushions which are lined with a specially prepared felt will insulate the walls and floors from many foundation transmitted noises.

Whether there is imminent danger of foundation rumbles or not, the floor of each room, both upstairs and down, can be given added noise protection by covering the sub flooring with a sound absorbing material before the finished flooring is laid.

And the noise of an electric mixer or of the home typewriter can be cut down by putting a sheet of sponge rubber
under their legs.

VI

If the house is already built the second principle should
be most used in the conquest of noise. This is the generous
—even lavish—use of sound absorbing materials. Ordinary plaster for all practical purposes does not absorb
noise. Old-fashioned hair plaster had some sound absorbing power, but try to buy some at your local building supply dealer's. There are now on the market special sound-
absorbing plasters, but they require the skill of specially
trained experts to apply.

When paneled walls are in harmony with the decorative
scheme and architectural design there are some wall boards
which are highly efficient in absorbing noise which can economically be used and applied by your local carpenter.
The use of these is highly desirable in hallways, sleeping
rooms, and children's rooms. If you are considering replas-
tering or redecorating any of these places it would be well to
investigate the sound absorbing properties of materials in
your local lumber yard.

VII

Here are some little details which are also worth
watching:

Curved wall surfaces should be avoided, since they focus
noises and produce a "whispering gallery" effect, making
some parts of the room noisier than others.

The larger the room, the longer the noises remain audible
in it. Low ceilings, which reduce the cubic dimensions,
make quieter rooms. So does a small floor area.

Linoleum or rubber tops on the kitchen work surfaces deaden the noise of utensils being slammed on them.

Double glass on the windows lessens greatly the amount of noise which comes in from outside, and also reduces the bill for winter heating.

Water, heating, and gas pipes should not be in direct contact with walls, since they will telegraph noises if they are. Where these pass through walls or floors they should have a clearance of one inch all around and have the open space packed with hair felt.

Door checks should be used to prevent the slamming of doors, and to make certain the doors are closed when the children are careless.

Door hinges can well be oiled several times a year to prevent squeaks.

VIII

The professional pessimists who think our civilization has reached the point of diminishing returns may be partially right. This is because our civilization has grown as a mechanical Moloch, while man himself has not improved in any basic way in the last twenty centuries. The pace of life has steadily increased, the environmental strains such as noise have also grown apace, giving a serious conflict between a mechanically improved environment and an unimproved mankind.

The middle portions of this book were devoted primarily to showing how the individual man or woman could strengthen and improve by their own intelligent efforts. The last section has shown how this same average person can also take control of some elements in their daily environment and use them as friendly forces for the furtherance of personal happiness and vocational success.

Adapting mankind and his present environment to each

other is a problem as difficult as it is important. I hope this book will serve to help you along the highway of happiness as you apply these suggestions for removing unnecessary strains on human nature, and adapting yourself inwardly to those forceful strains which cannot yet be eliminated.

"Never despair!"

—Motto of *Jonas Hanway*, English boy who became a merchant and philanthropist, and invented the first umbrella.

INDEX

Accidents, 247 f.
Adrenalin, 140
Aged, memory in, 106
Air-conditioning, 12 f., 271 ff.
Alcohol, 21 f., 107
Ambivert, 182 f.
Amnesia, 97
Anger, 137 ff.
Annoyance, 246 f.
Association, 81 ff.
Attention, 80
Attitude, 39
Automatic writing, 148

Bacon, Francis, 113 ff.
Bed, 237
Blues, 147
Breaking habits, 48
Bricklayers, 4

Climate, 12 f.
Coffee, 22, 223, 231 f.
Color, 268 f.
Compensation, 170
Cooling, 19
Country, 221
Cross-training, 36 f.
Curve of forgetting, 86

Day-dreams, 122 ff.
Delirium, 105
Digestion, 221 (*See also* Fear)
Distraction, 20
Dogs, 102
Dreams, 126 ff.

Egocentric personality, 155
Electricity, in home, 259 ff.
Embarrassment, 245 f.
Emotion, 137 ff., 181

Emotional, personality, 156 f.
Extrovert, 182 f.
Eye fatigue, 67
Eye movements, 67
Eyes, 11, 265 ff.

False memories, 98
Fatigue, 199 ff., 210 ff., 241 f.
Fear, 137 ff.
Fear reaction, 219 ff.
"Feel," 36
Food, 231 f., **234**
Forgetting, curve of, 86

General training, 37
Geniuses, 7
Ghosts, 99
Glass, ultra-violet, 279 f.
Glasses, eye, 11
Growth, 221

Habit, 43 ff., 174 f., 239
Habits, breaking, 48 f.
Heating, 271 ff.
Hour of day, 24 f.
House, tests of, 253 ff.
Humidity, 16 f., 273 f.
Hypnotism, 164 f.
Hysteria, 201

Iceberg, mental, 166
Idols, 113 ff.
Illumination, 8 ff., 259 ff., 265 ff.
Imagination, 96
Inadequate personality, 157
Inaudible speech, 132
Incentive, 38
Information, 116
Insomnia, 253 f.